Praise for Marianne Thompson's
Zapped: A True Story of Divine Intervention

"*Zapped* is a great story of synchronicity and daring. Marianne creates a good model for how to explore every event, investigate every meeting, and discover, always, the positive message—all while keeping a sense of humor."
—James Redfield, author of *The Celestine Prophecy*

"*Zapped: A True Story of Divine Intervention* is an engaging real-life story that looks at remarkable coincidences as discreet Divine Intervention. *Zapped* is a powerful modern parable as engaging and entertaining as it is meaningful and inspirational."
—Midwest Book Review

"*Zapped* is an astonishingly vivid portrait of spiritual awakening and self-discovery. I laughed, I cried, I couldn't stop reading."
—Reverend Anne Coffman

D0927368

Zapped

A True Story of
Divine Intervention

MARIANNE THOMPSON

WINTHROP HOUSE PUBLISHING
Greenwich, Connecticut

Winthrop House Publishing
P.O. Box 0037
Greenwich, Connecticut 06836
e-mail address: Winthrophousepub@aol.com

ISBN: 0-9710119-0-7
LCCN: 20011090523

Grateful acknowledgment is given to the following for
permission to reprint excerpts from the following:

Man's Search for Himself by Rollo May. Copyright © 1953
W.W. Norton & Company. Reprinted by permission of W.W.
Norton & Company.

Freedom and Destiny by Rollo May. Copyright © 1991 Rollo
May. Reprinted by permission of W.W. Norton & Company.

The Late Blooming Groom by Joan Kelly Bernard. Copyright
© 1994 Newsday, Inc. Reprinted by permission of Newsday,
Inc.

Medical Breakthrough by Diane Goldner. Copyright ©
Reprinted by permission of Diane Goldner.

Dedication

This is dedicated to Reverend Ron Allison. Without his support, encouragement and belief in my story this book would never have been completed.

This is also dedicated to the adult children of alcoholics, for I am one of you. For those of us who are struggling, if in any way this book helps you to gain love and compassion for yourself and what you had to endure during your childhood, then my efforts will have been well worth it.

ACKNOWLEDGEMENTS

With great thanks to the people who have donated hours of free time in editing all my errors and helping me put this book in order. With special thanks to Peggy Fischer, a woman whose exuberance and positive attitude pushed me to produce the best writing I could.

Thanks also to Eva Maria Palevich whose brilliant mind sparked the creation of the cover design. Kudos to Mary Lee McKenna for the editing of the original manuscript and to Tom Abbott for the final coat of polish. Also thanks to Tania Perez my fashion industry editor.

With gratitude to Betsy Campbell for her wonderful support throughout this project and for leading me to my wonderful, kind and extremely talented photographer, David Rosenblum. Also special thanks to Pat Reshen for her support in trying times and tremendous help with the manuscript. I thank you all from the bottom of my heart. Most importantly, I thank God for turning my life around and for all the wonderful true stories he gave me to write about. Now that's what I call great material.

AUTHORS NOTE

Swiss psychotherapist, Carl Jung, studied the role of 'meaningful coincidences' in our lives and coined the term "synchronicity" for those uncanny coincidences that are beyond mere chance. He taught us how to recognize their significance and utilize them as guides to the answers we are seeking.

It was after an intense period of prayer in asking God to help solve my problems when a series of powerful, guiding coincidences occurred that transformed my life. I discovered my true self.

To heal and become self-actualized, we must come to terms with the past. What I have learned from this experience is that many of our problems in adulthood stem from unresolved childhood conflicts that are linked to the traumatic events of the past. These unresolved conflicts are unconsciously carried into our adulthood and are directly related to our insecurities, over-reactions, neurotic and self-destructive behaviors.

Life takes on a new dimension with self-discovery when the excitement of finding your hidden talents and passions leads you to a whole new you.

The following is a true story. All the coincidences are true. All the incidents leading up to the coincidences are true. Approximately eighty percent of the dialogue is exact.

In the psychology sections, I have taken liberties with the dialogue for teaching purposes and also in chapters two and four for entertainment purposes. Some names have been changed to protect those involved.

Trust in the Lord with all thine heart;
And lean not unto thine own understanding. In all thy
ways acknowledge him, and he will direct thy paths.

Proverbs 3: 5-6

CONTENTS

SHUFFLING OFF TO PERU

The nurse led me to the examination room, placed my file in the holder on the door, pulled a crisp new sheet of paper over the examination table, handed me a hospital gown and said, "Remove your clothes, leaving on just your underwear."

The room was freezing. Goosebumps covered my arms as I climbed up on the cold table. "The doctor will be right in to see you..."

A half an hour later, he arrived.

He walked in, head down, reading my file and said, "Good afternoon, Ms. Thompson, it's been a while since I last saw you. How have you been feeling?"

"Not very well. My neck is out again."

"I see from my records that it's been seven years since I last saw you. You had two herniated discs, between C-4 and C-6. What are your symptoms now?"

"The same as last time. A constant pain in my neck that

sometimes radiates down my arm."

"Let's take a look at your MRI." He walked over to the light box on the wall, set the films on top, sat down and turned on the light. "Oh, wow!" He shook his head from side to side with jaw dropped.

"What do you see?" I asked nervously.

"Spinal cord compression."

"What does that mean?"

He walked over to the table I was sitting on, pulled up a stool, sat down and said, "It means that the discs are pressing on the spinal cord. Let's give you a physical. Turn your head to the right and then to the left."

I struggled as I barely turned my head from side to side. "Ow, it hurts," I said, feeling totally miserable.

He then took out that little tomahawk they use to test your reflexes. Tapped my elbows, then the right knee. All of a sudden my right knee shot straight up. "Gee, look at that." I said with a nervous laugh. "I almost hit you."

He looked up at me very seriously and said, "Hyper-reflexes."

I was starting to freak out. Feeling threatened by his manner, I asked, "What does this all mean?"

"It means that my physical exam shows me the same thing that the MRI did. You have spinal cord compression. Your condition hasn't gotten better over the past seven years, it's gotten worse. The only way to help you is by operating."

I could feel my face turning red. I was burning up, tears started to roll down my cheeks and my voice was shaking as I said, "But I don't want an operation."

He looked up at me very compassionately, and said, "I

know you don't. And I'm sorry I have to tell you this, but I would be remiss if I didn't. If this isn't taken care of you could damage your spinal cord. This is what you need. You must consider it."

"How long will I be out of work?"

"That depends on what you do for a living."

"I work for a dress manufacturer in the fashion industry as a production patternmaker. I am responsible for the fit of the garment. It's a technical job, which entails drafting paper patterns at a large table and looking down all day. Not good for the neck."

"Then you would be able to go back to work after about three months."

"THREE MONTHS?!" I shrieked.

"Your health is more important than your job."

"What exactly does the operation entail?"

"We would make an incision in the front of your neck, take the two discs out, and then screw a metal plate over the two vertebrae to keep them from moving."

"That sounds horrible! You have to make an incision in the front? Won't there be a scar?"

"A small one, but we usually cut in the folds of the neck so it's not that noticeable. Listen, I've performed hundreds of these operations. I do this all day long. There's nothing to worry about," he said with a wave of his hand, like this was no big deal.

No big deal for him. I couldn't believe his cavalier attitude. I felt like kicking him. Where's that tomahawk?

"Can't we treat this with medication instead?" I asked frantically.

"I'm sorry, the only answer is surgery. So, think about it and let me know. The procedure should be done within six weeks."

I boarded the subway in tears. What am I going to do? I can't have an operation. My neck hurts but the pain is not that severe. I can live with the pain; it's this spinal cord compression stuff that scares me. I have to get a second opinion.

The following morning, I walked into my boss's office to give him the update. "How did it go yesterday?" he asked.

I ran my index finger across my neck in a swift slicing motion, with sound effect and said, "Not good. He wants to cut me open. And I would be out of work for three months."

With a pained look on his face he said, "Sorry to hear that Marianne. Let me know what you decide to do."

I was totally depressed as I discussed my dilemma with my co-workers. Some told tales of successful operations of their own or those of friends. Others refused to go under the knife. In the end the decision had to be mine.

When I passed by my Peruvian co-worker, Jose´, he asked how I was feeling. "Horrible, they want to operate."

"Don't get an operation. They might make a mistake and you could wind up paralyzed." He then paused for a minute deep in thought and said, "You know, Marianne, you should go to Peru for an Inca healing."

"WHAT?! An Inca healing? Are you crazy?"

"No, really, I'm serious. In Peru when the doctors can't help people, they go to the healers."

I was amazed that he was actually suggesting this to me. Deciding to placate him, I asked, "How do I find out about these Inca healings?"

"Go to any library and search for books pertaining to shamanism. There will be lots of information on it, you'll see."

"Okay, I think I will. Why not?" I walked away thinking he's totally lost it. But, it does sound interesting so I'll investigate later.

During the day I started to fantasize... *Why not go for an Inca healing? Take a vacation in Peru to see if they can heal me and if it doesn't work I can always have a good old American operation. Inca healing. Doesn't sound so bad after all. I just might be wild and crazy enough to take old Jose' up on this Inca healing bit.*

That evening I boarded the 5:52 Metro North Commuter train to Greenwich, Connecticut. I entered the second car from the front as I usually do, and found an end seat facing the rear door.

A few seats down, I noticed a man and a woman talking to each other. I recognized them because they also always sit in this particular car. They are part of a group of friends that meets every night on this train to chat about current events, the Ally McBeal Show, etc. Personally I didn't know them and they didn't know me.

I was observing them. The man, facing me, was talking with the woman when suddenly he reached into his briefcase, which was on his lap, pulled out a book and placed it on top. He continued talking to the woman but began fidgeting with the book. He held it up and put it down. Then he held it up a second time so that the front cover was facing me. The title was...*Inca Gold.*

My heart was pounding and I was in utter shock. I couldn't believe it. What a bizarre coincidence. I was *Zapped!*

He didn't say anything to the woman about the book. A

few seconds later, he put it down. Another minute went by, he opened his briefcase and put it back inside. It seemed to be a totally unconscious act.

For the past six years, I have been experiencing these haunting coincidences. It all started after a two-month period of intense prayer when I asked God to help me solve my problems. A series of uncanny coincidences began to unfold that seemed to be guiding me to the answers I was looking for. It has been quite a journey.

I got home that night, turned on the computer, logged on the World Wide Web, typed in "shamanism" and pressed search. 462 sites for Inca healing shamanism! There must be something to this stuff.

There's a famous saying: "There's no such thing as a coincidence, it's just God's way of remaining anonymous."

I had to go to Peru.

It took a couple of months to get an appointment for my second opinion. This time I went to a top guy. I saw the Chief of Spinal Surgery at NYU Hospital. It was déjà vu with the cold examination room and long wait but his response was different.

"Many doctors would look at this MRI and say the discs have to come out. But I'm conservative. You're functioning, going to work every day. Your pain at this point is not that severe so I am not going to suggest surgery. My guess is that you will probably need it at some point in your life but not now. I'm sending you to a colleague of mine and he'll put you on anti-inflammatory medication and physical therapy."

Right Answer!

As the year progressed my neck was better for a while but continued to flare up periodically. I was popping anti-inflammatory pills like they were candy, but the pain was still there. I was sick of this constant nagging pain.

"I'm going to Peru."

"Are you crazy? You can't go to Peru. It's dangerous! There's an American woman in prison down there. She was falsely accused of trying to overthrow the government," my sister screamed into the phone.

"Well, I wasn't planning on overthrowing the government."

"Very funny. Stop fooling around. I'm serious. It's not safe there."

"Listen, New York can be dangerous, too. I wonder what the Peruvians think of us when they hear about the crime that takes place here. Besides, the place intrigues me. It's the hot vacation spot for New Age hippie types. I'm going to Peru and you can't stop me."

"Listen to your big sister, don't go!"

The State Department's Report on Peru suddenly appeared in my mailbox, with areas of interest highlighted. My big sister was on a mission. Yes, there is an American in jail there and pick-pocketing is also a problem, but I was pick pocketed in New York. The report didn't scare me nor impress me.

I enlisted my Cuban friend, Maritza, to accompany me on my journey. Not only is she a good friend, she speaks Spanish. *Mucho importante.* It took about a year and two months for the trip to materialize.

But by the time we were set to go, my neck was fine. I had started taking this Joint Repair System from General

Nutrition Center a few months earlier and I hadn't had any pain since. The system consists of completely natural nutritional supplements in pill form. It really was a miracle because prior to this I was ready to go for another MRI. I was in chronic pain, couldn't sleep at night, and the anti-inflammatory pills weren't working anymore. I was definitely ready for an Inca Healing. Now I didn't need one but I was still interested in the subject.

On July 1, 2000, we took off from New York's LaGuardia Airport on American Airlines headed for Peru.

It took us eight hours to get to Miami.

We were off to a bad start. The Miami airport was closed due to thunderstorms. We circled the airport and then had to head to the Bahamas to refuel. With no food and nothing but water to drink, we sat in the airplane for hours and waited until they got the okay from Miami that the airport was open. When we finally arrived in Miami, we had missed our connecting flight, our luggage was missing and we had to wait in line for three hours to reschedule our flight.

I began to daydream about one of those vacations where you just stay home and clean out your closets.

They put us up in a hotel and the next morning we once again headed for Peru. I was getting excited about the trip. We would land in Lima, the capital, spend the night there and then take off the next day for Cuzco, ancient city of the Incas, spend a few nights there and then to Machu Picchu, Peru's biggest tourist attraction.

I was to contact José's sister Sulma when I arrived in Cuzco. She was going to hook me up with an Inca healer. Sulma is a schoolteacher who lives and works in Cuzco.

We arrived in Lima without a hitch and our luggage was

waiting for us at Lima International Airport. Thank you, Lord.

The ride from the airport to our hotel in Miraflores was appalling. As I looked out the grimy window of the taxi I realized how lucky I am to be an American. The depth of the poverty in this section of Lima was overwhelming. Row after row of these crumbling, single story concrete structures set upon dirt. There was no grass. I saw very few trees in this area. "Are those homes, Maritza?"

"Oh my God, yes, they are homes."

I'd never seen anything like it. Some of the structures had makeshift doors, windows without glass. Off to the side we saw people washing their clothes in a river that looked filthy. The gas stations were primitive. The convenience stores were shacks with hand-painted signs listing the products they sold inside. Fumes encased the city. There was no escaping the putrid smells that flowed in and out of the cab. Massive displays of graffiti were everywhere. Buildings were plastered with signs "Toledo el Presidente´."

Maybe my big sister was right.

The scenery was much improved as we entered Miraflores, which is supposed to be Lima's most important shopping, entertainment and residential area.

We were booked to stay at the Hotel Aristo, listed in the travel guide as a place to stay at the top end. I guess top end in Peru means the rooms are clean and adequate and the area is safe to walk around in at night.

We went to bed at 9:00 p.m. that night. We had to be at the airport at 6:00 a.m. for our flight to Cuzco. That was the only flight we could get on since our original plans were screwed up from the Miami disaster.

We arrived at the Hotel Monesterio in Cuzco and it was

beautiful. This is a five star hotel built on the site of an Inca Palace. It was originally a 16th century monastery. The gardens in the central courtyard were just breathtaking.

The narrow, steep streets of Cuzco are often lined with massive Inca-built stonewalls. The people are a mix of Spanish Peruvian and Quechua-speaking Indians who are descendants of the Incas.

We checked our bags and when we walked outside the hotel there was a family of Indians in colorful native dress sitting by the fountain with a Llama!

One of the women had a beautiful baby on her lap, dressed in a multicolored Inca style knit cap and patchwork dress of brilliant colors. But she was filthy. They were so poor.

"Picture, Miss?" she asked in broken English.

"Of course I'd like a picture." This was wild. I sat down in front of the family and Maritza snapped away. When we were finished they stretched their hands out looking for money. I was happy to give them money, I felt so bad for them.

Cuzco was a contrast of beauty and poverty. Stunning architecture, magnificent churches, bustling streets filled with merchants selling exotic wares, throngs of native Inca Indians in customary dress.

I called Sulma when we got back to the hotel and we had arranged to have coffee and dessert that evening. She was a petite woman with black shoulder length hair and tanned skin. Her clothing was worn and the black leather on her pocketbook was so tattered it looked like she bought it twenty years ago. She looked poor, but probably was considered middle class by Peruvian standards.

She told me her friend Alberto had given her the name

of a coca leaf reader who lived in a town outside of Cuzco. If I wanted to go she was available on Wednesday afternoon.

Well, I really didn't want to see a coca leaf reader. I wanted to see an Inca healer. But, what the hell, I might as well hear what he has to say.

She picked me up at the hotel in a taxicab. Now in Peru, you can hire a taxi for three hours and it only costs ten dollars. They'll drive you where you want to go, wait outside for an hour or so, and then take you home. No meters in Peru.

Sulma instructed the driver to go to the town of Huasao, which is about twenty minutes outside Cuzco. When we got to the town we were supposed to stop and ask a local where this coca leaf reader lived.

The poverty level increased as we left the city. The Indians that live in the surrounding towns build their homes from the earth. They make sun-dried adobe bricks from the soil which is a deep reddish clay. Then with these clay bricks they construct one story rectangular homes that have either a flat corrugated metal or thatched roof. A super deluxe version has windows with glass. Most have no windows. The doors may consist of a piece of plywood or a rough sheet of metal that is somehow hinged into the clay. When they build enough of these homes in an area, the government will give them running water and perhaps electricity.

I was on another planet.

The cab driver mistakenly passed the town and we had to backtrack. I decided to tell Sulma about the book I had written.

"I wrote a book, Sulma, about the concept of meaningful coincidence. It's a true story, about a series of Divine coincidences that guided me into a personal transformation.

"At the time, I was a woman who didn't know her own self worth, floating in and out of depression with a slew of disastrous personal relationships trailing behind. Anxiety followed me everywhere.

"Through the power of prayer, and the resulting occurrence of these guiding coincidences, I was able to conquer my demons. As a matter of fact it was a coincidence that brought me to Peru," I said.

I then went into detail about Jose´ urging me to go for the Inca Healing, and the strange coincidence on the train. I also went into more detail about the previous series of coincidences that guided me into this transformation.

"Ninety-eight percent of the people who read my book loved it. They rave about it. They cry. They laugh. 'Never give up,' they tell me. But it is so difficult for an unpublished author to get published. I've been trying to get published for the last four years! I need an agent to get to the publisher. And agents don't want to deal with unpublished authors. Catch-22. It's so frustrating. So, maybe the coca leaf reader can help me with my book," I said, feeling rather hopeless.

 The cab finally reached the town and Sulma hopped out and went to knock on the door of one of these clay huts. I couldn't believe she did this. She didn't know any of the people in this town. I was feeling rather uneasy at this point.

She came back to the cab and said that the people told her the man whose name Alberto had given her was not in town today. "Just go down the street and ask one of the locals. There are a couple of other coca leaf readers in town," they said.

We made a right turn onto a dirt road, filled with huge

bumps, mud, and deep crevices filled with water. I couldn't believe the cab was driving up this road. I didn't think he was going to make it.

What am I doing here?

I was getting very nervous.

We stopped and asked a local boy and he told us to make the next right and look for the house with the coca leaves on the door. We made the right and spotted the house. A clay adobe hut that had a metal sheet for a door. Three coca leaves were painted on the top of the door. The cab driver parked the car and Sulma got out and knocked on the door.

I was standing a few feet away thinking, this is crazy! I can't do this. I live in Greenwich, Connecticut! What am I doing here?

"Sulma, let's go. I don't think we should do this." I started to panic.

"You've come this far. Please, he's coming," she said waving me on.

Well, the cab driver's here. If anything happens, we'll scream and he'll come rescue us. I arrived at the front door just as the man opened it. He was an Indian man probably in his early forties, dressed in a plaid flannel shirt with a tee shirt under it, dusty blue pants, and work boots.

"Come in," he said.

We stepped into this clay hut and I couldn't believe what I saw. It was a large room with a dirt floor. There was no roof over this portion of the house.

The sunroof effect.

There was a pig in one corner nursing her litter of eight baby pigs. There was another pig in the other corner. There was a chicken with baby chicks running around. There was a second man sitting on a bench against the wall. He was eating something out of a bowl. There was what appeared to be some sort of kitchen area. No Whirlpool or Amana here. There was a pot cooking over an open flame.

I was in shock.

There was no furniture. There was no electricity. I doubt they had running water.

"We're eating our lunch, you're going to have to wait," he told Sulma. "You can wait in the other room," he said, pointing to a room to the right.

We entered this room and at this point I was a nervous wreck. This is nuts.

This room had a roof of plastic sheets and hay. The right side of the room had a wooden table against the wall covered with a colorful lightweight Indian rug. There were coca leaves on top of the table and two benches on either side of the table. There was a dried up dead condor displayed on the left wall behind the table.

Their taxidermy skills do need improving.

Behind the table was a painting of two condors. To the right was his sleeping bag laid on top of a pile of hay.

The wall straight ahead of me had a picture of Christ, a vase with flowers, trinkets of some sort. It looked like a gypsy setup. There was a huge newspaper article plastered to the wall.

"Look, he's famous," Sulma said as she began to read and translate the newspaper article. "It says here that he can predict the future. He is very well known in Peru."

There were also two certificates hanging on the wall pertaining to his psychic ability.

On the left wall there were the skins of a skunk, a deer and some other unidentifiable animal.

We sat down on the bench and a minute later he entered. He smiled, shook our hands and sat down on the bench behind the table. I said nothing to him. The first thing he said was, "Many Americans come here."

"Oh really. Any famous Americans?" I asked.

"Yes," he said. He then started to look through a small journal that was on his right. He pulled out a business card and handed it to me. It was a business card from a woman in Massachusetts. Linda Matthews...EDITOR/PUBLISHER.

"Oh my God!! I can't believe it." I sat there shaking in utter shock. "Sulma! This is a business card of an EDITOR/PUBLISHER!"

"It's Another Coincidence!!" she shrieked.

"*Zapped* again!" I exclaimed. I nervously jotted down Linda's address and telephone number. I knew I would call her as soon as I got back to the States...

An Indian in Peru, sitting in his clay adobe hut, handed me this business card and finally, after five years of excruciating labor, my baby was born.

Zapped

A True Story of Divine Intervention

LAST CALL IN MANHATTAN

April 1993

I walked over to my bedroom window, pushed back the lace curtains and could see the traffic coming off the Queensboro Bridge. As I looked down First Avenue, I felt like sticking my head out the window and shouting, "I'm sick and tired of this and I'm not going to take it anymore!"

My God, I've been living the single life in Manhattan for eleven years and I still haven't hooked up with that one special guy. It seems to be harder to find a husband in this city than it is to climb Mount Everest in the nude.

I fluffed my pillow, flopped my head down feeling totally baffled by my situation. I just couldn't figure it out.

I am considered to be very attractive, slim, fashionable, and smart. I don't have a problem meeting men. I just don't meet the right men. Short-term relationships are my specialty. Is it the city or is it me? I feel like a psycho magnet.

Actually, living in Manhattan was a single woman's dream for a while. Just a step outside my apartment and the city was at my beck and call. The nightlife in New York can't be beat. My friends and I have probably hit every club in this city from happy hours to wee hours and on to after hours. We've been uptown girls, downtown girls, eastside and westside girls scouring the city for Mr. Wonderful. Oh, we've had a few nibbles here and there but as it stands, we're still empty handed.

Don't get me wrong, I've had some great times in this city, but some extremely lonely ones as well. I just don't understand why I have a problem forming lasting relationships. You would think with all the people in Manhattan, it would be easy to find someone special. But the city can be very isolating. You almost become like a rat in a maze living in this city, going from your apartment to the office, to the health club, and to your few favorite restaurants and watering holes. Over the years I've become such a creature of habit.

At least I finally found the courage to pry myself out of this rut. This was to be my last weekend living in the city.

I rolled over, yawned, closed my eyes and was ready to take a much-needed nap when the phone rang.

"Hi Marianne, this is Christine. Did I wake you?"

"No, I was getting ready to take a little snooze but I haven't lost consciousness yet."

"So how did you like your last big night out on the town?"

"I'm sure it won't be my last, just the last one while living in the city. It was a great time. The dinner at Dock's was fabulous and so were the drinks. Too many drinks. I have the energy level of a slug today, but we sure did have fun. That was so nice of you and Beth to give me a little going away party. I'm going to miss you both."

"It's not like you're moving to California. Greenwich is very close to the city. We'll still hang out together, it's just that now we'll have two places to hang instead of only one. I hope the man situation is better there than it is in New York."

"It's got to be better. It can't be any worse. I wonder what the men in Greenwich will be like."

"Well, it's the Wasp Capital of the World and the people in the area have a reputation of being rather snobbish and upper crusty. I wonder if those wealthy preppies are good in bed."

"Christine! Don't be so crude! I know their personalities are stereotyped as being rather formal and...stiff, so I'm sure they'll be just fine!"

Christine laughed and said, "Alright, enough of the man-talk. I know you're going to love the town. It's absolutely gorgeous and the place is crawling with celebrities."

"You know I've been doing some research on the town and you wouldn't believe the Who's Who list of famous people who live and have lived in Greenwich. Stars of stage and screen. Glenn Close grew up in Greenwich. Actually, her ancestors were among the founders of Greenwich. Henry Fonda lived in Greenwich for many years. And one of my favorites who's now gone, The Great and Powerful Oz, Frank Morgan, the wizard himself! And currently mega-hunk Mel Gibson lives in Greenwich and Paul Newman nearby in Westport."

"Wow, I didn't realize the list was that extensive."

"Oh the list doesn't stop there. On the political scene

we have George Bush who grew up about a half-mile from where I'll be living. And we have scores of ambassadors and even a Saudi Princess and the widow of the Shah of Iran."

"So many famous people! There must be some infamous as well."

"Oh sure. The one and only Leona Helmsley. Remember, she was convicted for tax evasion in 1989 and served 18 months in federal prison. She was quoted as saying, 'Only the little people pay taxes.' Can you believe that? She has a huge estate in the backcountry of Greenwich. Some call it the *House of Greed*, but lately she has been very generous, donating the funds for a huge wing to be added to Greenwich Hospital. I guess she had a lot to think about while making those license plates in the pen.

"But the most unsettling of the infamous is the Skakel family. Ethel Skakel married Robert F. Kennedy at St. Mary's Church, which is right on Greenwich Avenue, a few blocks from my apartment. There are rumors about Michael and Tommy Skakel, Ethel's nephews, being involved with the murder of Martha Moxley, the then 15- year-old girl who lived next door. That happened about twenty years ago."

"That's really scary. And to think he came from such a prominent family. Well, it sure looks like Greenwich has a stockpile of notable figures."

"It really is unbelievable. The list goes on and on."

"I'm so excited for you. You're going to love Greenwich. I just hope you don't forget your friends in New York."

"How could I forget my best friends? I'm expecting you both to come out for the weekend. Soon!" I said, hoping I made the right decision in moving.

"Don't worry; we'll be out in a week or two. I can't wait

to see the new place. Good luck with the move tomorrow."

Geez, it's four o'clock already, there's no time to take a nap, and the movers are coming tomorrow. I climbed out of bed, and went back to packing. As I began dusting off books and carefully packing them into boxes, my mind lapsed into a daydream. I began to wonder if I was going to miss New York. I probably will miss some things, but I think I overstayed my welcome in Manhattan. I've just been here too long so I am really excited about settling in Greenwich. Land of the Rich and Famous. Hollywood of the East Coast. Yes, this is going to be a very interesting move.

The alarm went off at nine o'clock and I slowly lifted my head off my pillow. I dressed and began preparing my mind for the tough day I had ahead of me.

The intercom buzzed. "Hello."

"This is the moving company. We're here to start the job."

I opened the door to two men, one towering over the other. They began carrying boxes down and since they were being paid by the hour, they slowly loaded up the truck. They also had to lock up the truck with every run to prevent any slimy thieves from ripping anything off during the move. It took more time to do it that way, but that's the way of life in this city. You have to be on guard at all times.

When the movers loaded the last box onto the truck, I gave them directions and told them to follow me. I started the car and headed toward the FDR Drive and then onto I-95 North to New England. Greenwich is situated just 30 miles north. This makes it an ideal commute. After about forty minutes of driving, we reached Exit 3, Arch Street, Greenwich. I pulled off the exit ramp and entered an entirely different world.

We made the turn onto Grigg Street and parked in front of my building. It's a brick pre-war structure built in 1938 so it has plenty of that art-deco charm with high ceilings, crown moldings, and parquet floors. It's gorgeous. As soon as the realtor showed it to me, I fell in love with it. The place is a little more expensive than my apartment in New York but I can't believe how huge it is. My new foyer is the same size as the bedroom I used to have. Overall, the place is twice the size of the little shoebox I had been living in.

The movers opened up the truck, started to unload, and just as John, the big guy, was about to lock up the truck for the first run into the apartment, he looked down the street, saw the police officer directing traffic, shook his head, turned to his partner and said, "We don't have to lock up here."

Instead of getting down to the drudgery of unpacking, I decided to explore the avenue. Greenwich Avenue, compared with Rodeo Drive by some, is very cosmopolitan but at the same time very quaint.

Greenwich is a Colonial town settled in 1640. It looks very similar to the Hamptons out on the east end of Long Island. Many of the buildings that stand now were constructed in the 1800's to early 1900's. These are structures of ornate concrete and brick no more than four or five stories high with many of them deemed historic landmarks by the town.

The finest shops and trendy boutiques occupy the

ground floors of these buildings. Saks Fifth Avenue, Baccarat, Tiffany's, as well as American classics, The Gap, Banana Republic, and Pier One.

Galleries, and restaurants are also abundant. It's a bit of a Restaurant Row with fifteen places to dine on a mile long strip.

As I continued to walk up the avenue in a semiconscious gaze taking in all of this luxury, I was abruptly stopped as I started to cross the street. "Step back onto the curb, Miss," the uniformed policeman ordered.

Startled, I stepped back, looked around and noticed clusters of people on the corners watching the cop direct traffic. He then signaled the cars to move forward and a minute later stopped them, smiled at the pedestrians, and said, "Cross." Oh my God, I can't believe this. In Greenwich the police officers tell the pedestrians when to cross.

I feel like I've just entered the Twilight Zone, another dimension in time and space, in the town that's just too... *perfect*.

Demento Garmentos

The view was outstanding, as I walked down Greenwich Avenue to catch the train to New York. The cherry trees were in bloom and huge flowerbeds of brilliant tulips lined the sidewalks. An antique clock tower stands toward the bottom of the Avenue; flower baskets hung from the street lamps. It is a beautiful town.

I boarded the 8:01 express to Grand Central and found a spot in the middle of a three-seater which was a little cramped but at least I didn't have to stand. As the train rattled from side to side, I noticed most of my fellow commuters had their noses buried in *The New York Times*, although there were a few typing on their laptop computers and some catching up on the sleep they lost the night before. The car was so quiet. Nobody talked. There was complete silence.

The train plodded into the station where bottlenecks of commuters were trying to get off the platform. I glanced at my watch realizing that from now on I would have to take an earlier train to make it to the office on time. I work for Megan Scott, which is a company that manufactures moderately priced dresses in the wonderful world of fashion. I'm being sarcastic when I say wonderful.

I walked at a brisk pace, picked up a bagel and coffee on the way. It was 9:05 when the receptionist buzzed me into the office. As I passed by my boss Joe's office, I heard, "Good *afternoon*, Marianne." Being already out of his sight, I rolled my eyeballs, grimaced and said, "Good morning, Joe." For Christ's sake this guy will never give anyone a break when it comes to being late, even if it's only five minutes.

I strolled down the hall and when I passed the office of Kathy, the designer, I peeked in to say "hi."

"Hello! How was your first weekend in Greenwich?" she asked with her usual enthusiasm.

"Greenwich is great. I spent most of the weekend unpacking and just exploring the town."

"I'm sure you'll meet lots of people. A single woman living in Greenwich. How exciting."

Kathy is the nicest designer I ever worked for and such a doll, which is a rarity in this industry because the insecurity of the position often makes most of them very bitchy. I've become great friends with Kathy and often we trade war stories about the industry. The fashion industry, although it sounds very glamorous, is for the most part far from it. It's the hiring and firing capital of the world. Largest revolving door this side of the Mississippi.

I've put in sixteen unbelievable years so far. Oh, that's not sixteen years with one firm, No, Nooooo---I've had sixteen jobs in sixteen years!

As the famous fashion photographer Francesco Scavullo

once said, "In the fashion industry, they treat you like a tissue. They pick you up, use you, and then throw you away."

Perfect Analogy.

I also designed during my first five years working in the industry and I was really quite good at it, but the unscrupulous character I was then working for broke my spirit. His name was Steve. I started with the firm as an assistant designer and he gave me the opportunity to design which was the only nice thing he did for me, but even that was very self-serving on his part. I suppose I'm sounding bitter. Well, too bad, I am. Steve was one of three partners, Steve, Ira and Ken. The Three Stooges. The firm's name was Art Max Fashions.

Stooge number two, Ken, was a 400-pound, vile, immoral excuse of a man. I'll never forget the time he was selling dresses in the showroom when one of the buyers noticed some white powder under his nose. It was cocaine, of course.

Another addict.

The industry was filled with them in the early eighties. Anyway, when the buyer asked him what the white powder was, he said, "Oh that must be from the powdered donut I just ate. It was the best donut I ever had."

And last but not least we had Ira, a classic garmento who spent ninety percent of the day screaming his head off. Ira was the oldest of the three being around fifty with graying hair, probably given to him by Steve and Ken. I suppose he was the smartest of the three, but his Type A personality made for a lot of rough riding through the ups and downs of day-to-day business.

The Three Stooges were always fighting and Steve seemed particularly unhappy. As it turned out, a few

months later, Steve dissolved his partnership with Ken and
Ira and got a gig with a sportswear manufacturer. He called
me at home the night of the breakup to ask me if I wanted
to go with him. At the time, he was the only one of the three
who was nice to me, and we really made a pretty good design team. So I told him he had a deal and gave notice to
Ken and Ira the next day.

We arrived on the scene of the new sportswear firm.
Then six months later he wanted out. He was offered a partnership at another company called T.J. and Co., so once
again as his steady companion, yours truly packed up and
moved with him, which, though stressful, was really fine for
me since I wasn't happy at the new company either.

We arrived at T.J. and Co., a dying division of a larger
firm, and were expected to resurrect this company from the
dead. We certainly had our work cut out for us, since a new
completed spring line had to be finished in a couple of
weeks. I frantically put together the line, sketching and designing at home and then putting in a full day at the office
drafting the first patterns. Needless to say I was exhausted.
But Steve kept saying, "Stick with me baby and you'll be in
diamonds. You'll get everything you want including an assistant and a raise."

The line was a hit! One month after we started, the buying offices were sending a newsletter to all their specialty
stores across the country with nothing but rave reviews for
the new line at T.J. and Co., telling the store that this was a
must shop. I was thrilled and so proud of what I had accomplished. The line was so successful, they opened another division soon after, a better line, selling dresses made
of more expensive cloth and better quality labor. I was excited but I really was running low on energy, losing sleep,

staying up later and later with all the sketching I had to do at home. I was exhausted. I kept telling Steve I wanted to hire an assistant. I needed help.

In August, I was off to Europe with my sister for pleasure and also for business since Steve wanted me to shop the stores for new ideas. Usually the company will send the designer to Europe with all the funds needed to pick up new styles to copy. He didn't give me a dime, just told me to sketch away while vacationing.

I came back with plenty of new ideas and I also came back to plenty of disappointments. Steve had hired an assistant for me while I was away and when I arrived back at the office he told me to teach her everything I knew. The whole thing made me very uncomfortable so I went to the office to discuss some of these issues. When I passed by the cartons of new labels for T.J. and Co., I noticed the label read, "Designed by Lisa Star." I couldn't believe it! Whose name was on the label? I spent my nights designing the new line and this is what I got and on top of everything else I found out from the new assistant, whom I should have hired, that Steve had taken all the credit for designing the line. I was livid.

I walked into the office, sat down, and said, "Who is Lisa Star and why is her name on the label?"

"Will you relax, it's just a buyer's name. We were having fun," he replied without a care in the world and with absolutely no regard for my feelings.

"Relax! How can I relax? I have spent many a sleepless night designing that line. I come back from Europe and I have a new assistant. I should have at least been involved in the hiring of my assistant. Then I find a strange name on the label. Every designer dreams of having her name on the label, and after all I have done this is how you treat me. How could you do this to me Steve?"

"If you're so unhappy, why don't you just leave," he replied smugly.

"You got it!" I said, leaving the room.

He just had no consideration, he never did. I guess part of it was due to his cocaine habit; you could always catch him in some corner of the place taking a hit or two. But I think it went beyond his cocaine habit. He was also a pathological liar, a cheat and a thief. Rumor had it that the Three Stooges had orgies in the office all the time, hiring prostitutes left and right. They also set the place on fire once and staged a robbery of their own trucker; scared the guy half to death, but the insurance companies paid off well. The list goes on and on. But, for some strange reason I thought Steve was different.

After I left the firm I went into a deep depression. All the running around, trying to find a place to settle into, all the hope of succeeding and when I finally thought I had, I was treated as though I didn't even count. Shortly thereafter, I stopped designing. Maybe I had given up too easily, but I lost my drive and without that, it's very hard to be creative. I had heard all the horror stories of how manufacturers just get tired of their designers and are always looking for "new blood". I didn't want to be a part of that scene any more, so I geared myself toward the technical end in hopes of becoming a production patternmaker. That was eleven years ago.

As I walked into my workroom, I mentally prepared myself for the busy day ahead. I had to make a tremendous number of patterns and quickly. Maria, my sample hand who sewed my garments, was setting up the iron for the day, filling it with water and turning it on.

Harry, the sample cutter, was clearing off his table in order to cut the new pattern I gave him yesterday and Ida, my fellow patternmaker, was sitting at her table stirring her coffee. Ida, an older woman in her sixties, has survived in this business for forty years. Don't ask me how. She looked up and said, "Good morning Marianne! How is the commuting going?"

"It's okay, I guess, I'll have to take an earlier train though. Joe was giving me his "Good afternoon" routine when I arrived five minutes late."

"Oh, he's unbelievable. He never gives us a break and now he has someone new to pick on. I hear a new patternmaker is starting today," Ida said.

"Gee, I wonder how long this one will last. This place is becoming a real revolving door lately. We must have had four patternmakers come and go in the last four months," I said, shaking my head.

"I know. It's unbelievable. Nobody seems to be fitting in lately."

"This is a crazy business. When I stopped designing and became a production patternmaker, I thought I would have more job security but that doesn't seem to be the case. Well, I have been here for three and a half years. That seems to be a landmark for me. What about you, Ida, how many jobs have you had?"

"At least a hundred. Once I received ten W-2 tax statements for the year!"

"Gee, the most I ever had was three. That's enough for me."

I started to draft my next pattern and thought about all the unbelievable experiences I'd had in this business. The industry is like something out of Hollywood with a never-ending string of crazy stories and bizarre characters. The world of fashion is a volatile, transient, fast-paced industry that is basically run by Jews and Italians. The main characters range from the mobsters who either own companies or shake down the other companies and the Jewish business owners who oblige them. One way or another the mob has its tax on every garment that is sold in this country. Estimates are that about 25 cents per gar- ment goes to the mob. That's a tremendous amount of money when you add up the millions of garments that are produced every year.

Personally I will not work for a company I know is owned by the mob, but one time I unknowingly wound up in just that position. I worked for a firm called Stargazer and my bosses were a group of fun guys in their mid-thirties, most of them Italian but I didn't think they were connected until one day when the "behind-the-scenes" owner walked in. I immediately raised an eyebrow when Mark, the production man, greeted the owner, Mr. Pappagallo, by kissing him on both cheeks. Something looked suspicious. I smelled a Godfather.

The following day I ran into one of the contractors who serviced the firm and we began to chat. "Ben, by the way, is Pappagallo..." I then put my forefinger to my nose squishing it to the left. The broken nose symbol for the mob.

"Are you kidding me?" he replied, adding, "Don't you know who he is? His brother Johnny was gunned down in Long Beach."

"Oh my God, I'm working for Al Capone and I didn't even know it."

"Oh they're not going to bother you. Don't worry about it," he replied and then went on his way.

Well, I didn't worry about it, but six months later I was worried when the company went out of business. Here I was on the road again, looking for a new job, which was now becoming a yearly occurrence. If they didn't go out of business, I was sexually harassed and had to leave, and I'm talking sexually harassed.

There's one bastard who sticks out in my mind. And these people are in my mind; permanently registered, they have left their indelible mark, a scar that can never be erased. Anyway, this shithead extraordinaire was a real tyrant of a boss, always yelling and screaming, flying off the handle over nothing. A real son-ofa- bitch. One day he called me over to discuss an error he found on my pattern and when I arrived at his workstation, he turned to me, smirked, said hello and then pinched my tit!

"I don't believe you Tony! Keep your hands off me!" I screamed on top of my lungs, face turning red and heart pounding so hard I thought my chest was going to explode.

"What are you talking about?" he said calmly, "I was just taking a thread off your sweater."

"Don't you ever touch me again!" I walked away in disgust.

What a bastard that guy was. Of course I had to leave the job, but I filed a complaint against the company and was awarded a few thousand dollars from the Division of Human Rights. I only wish I had retained a private attorney. I was told years later that I could have easily gotten twenty grand since the incident came under the heading of "assault". The industry was something else back then. Now with the laws protecting women things are a little better, but it still goes on.

I guess you're wondering why I don't get out, pack it in

and leave the industry. That's a task that's a lot easier said than done. When I graduated from The Fashion Institute of Technology, I left there with a heart full of dreams and hopes. I wanted to be a fashion designer which I did become and I was good at it; I succeeded but the people I wound up with broke my spirit, crushed and trampled on it. So I picked myself up, changed direction, found a new avenue in the industry, doing work that I enjoyed, but again my somewhat healed spirit was once more torn into little pieces, and before I knew it sixteen years had gone by. I was making good money, had only one marketable skill, and I was trapped in the Cesspool of Seventh Avenue. Holy Shit!

To find a home, a place where you can work peacefully, with just a smattering of job security seems to be nearly impossible. For the most part, the place I work now, Megan Scott, hasn't been too bad, but you can never really trust anyone you work for in this industry. You always have to watch your back and after years of this insecurity and abuse, one develops an affliction known as Garment Center Paranoia, with the only cure being a change of careers!

There is one nice aspect to working in the industry. Most of the jobs are gotten by word of mouth. The industry is a little Peyton Place. The fit models who work with me on the fitting and correcting of garments, work on a free-lance basis, usually by the hour, going from one manufacturer to the next. All the dress firms are in one or two buildings and all the sportswear manufacturers are in another set of buildings. There are about 3,500 manufacturers in New York, with most of them located on either Seventh Avenue or Broadway.

During their stops from manufacturer to manufacturer, the fit models as well as all the trimming, button and sales people pick up all the gossip as well as information as to what positions are open with the various manufacturers. Therefore, if your reputation is good, you shouldn't really have a problem finding a job through either your fit model or the sales people who service your firm; they'll get you a job just as fast as you lost your last one. But, if you've been screwing up a lot, or have recently made a huge mistake that messed up production, watch out. Your reputation can be easily damaged. As the saying goes, "If you fart on Seventh Avenue, they smell it on Broadway."

BRETT'S

We made our way through the crowd, eyeing the men on the way, smiling at the ones who caught our interest.

The dance floor was crammed as the music vibrated through one of the hottest spots in Fairfield County, Brett's, in the heart of Greenwich, Connecticut. "This place is packed tonight, Pam," I said to my cousin as I made my way to the bar to order our drinks. "It's Friday night. Time to let loose and P-A-R-T-Y!" she said scanning the crowd as I turned to Jigs, the bartender and put in an order for two Vodka and Cranberry.

Pam was instrumental in getting me to move to Greenwich, and I'm thankful for her company because she is the only soul I know in this town. It makes moving to a new area easier when you have someone to buzz around town with. Making new friends is not easy with the busy lifestyles people have today, so unless you can connect with someone who also needs to make new friends, it can be an arduous process settling in a new town.

Pam, who is nine years younger than I, is a friendly, chatty, very feminine type of girl, who is nice most of the time, but at other times can drive me absolutely bonkers. She has a sense of humor that specializes in cheap shots and constant digs that at times have me going for her jugular.

Jigs is the star bartender at Brett's. He has a traditional handlebar mustache, a great smile and a funny giggle when he tells a joke. He always makes you feel right at home whether he's joking around, listening to your woes or ringing the famous bell after getting a generous tip. Brett's is like a "Cheers" bar. A charming restaurant set in a renovated Victorian house with white columns on either side of the entrance and geranium-filled window boxes lining the perimeter of the dining room. The dark wood wainscoting, stained glass accents behind the mahogany bar and eclectic artwork give the place a warm, homey, pub-like atmosphere. At night the tables in the bar area are cleared away for dancing, the band sets up and you hear some of the best entertainment in the area. The crowd starts to pile in from nine-thirty on, usually four deep at the bar.

"Pam, see that good looking guy at the other end of the bar? I'd like to talk to him. Let's make our way over there," I said as I handed a drink to her and began squeezing my way through the crowd. I reached my intended destination and lucky me, there was a seat right next to the target of my affection. I sat down next to him, smiled, and felt I had hit the bull's-eye. God, he was good looking. Tall, tanned, dressed in khaki shorts, Polo shirt, and Topsiders.

I then turned to my cousin and nonchalantly started a conversation. "So, how did your week go?"

"Fine. Nothing much is new. You're the one with all the excitement in her life. How's the apartment coming along? And how do you like living in Greenwich compared to Manhattan?"

"The apartment is great. It's twice the size of the little shoebox I called home in Manhattan. I've got most things in order but still have a few boxes to unpack. And Greenwich is a beautiful town. Everything you could possibly need is in this town. You never have to leave. But it's almost too perfect. It's spooky."

As I finished my sentence, Mr. Bull's-eye started to laugh. He was obviously eavesdropping on our conversation.

"Well, it's true. This town is too perfect. On the surface that is," I said trying not to drool at the sight of this man.

"You're right. By the way, my name is Bill Williams," he said as he extended his hand out to shake.

"My name is Marianne Thompson and this is my cousin Pam Easton." We all shook hands and began talking. Bill and I started flirting and bantering back and forth. About a half hour had gone by when Pam spotted a friend across the bar and told me she would catch up with me later. Bill asked if I wanted another drink and I said "yes." After all it was Friday night. Pretty soon we were on the dance floor. We danced through the set, working up a sweat until we decided we had had enough.

"This band is great, isn't it?" I asked as we made our way back to our seats.

"They're my favorite. The horn section is fabulous, and the vocals superb. I was driving back from the city when I heard on the radio that Funkestra was playing, I came right over."

I sat down in my seat, took a sip of my drink and noticed an older man with wavy white hair heading our way. He had a martini in his left hand and a cigarette in his right. He also was wearing khaki shorts, a Polo shirt and Topsiders. The Uniform of Greenwich.

He smiled as he approached us and in a very upper crusty accent, said, "Bill, how are you doing and who is this pretty young lady you're with?"

"Winslow! How the hell are you? What a surprise." The men shook hands and then Bill said, "This is Marianne Thompson."

"Pleased to meet you. Winslow Barrett," he said, extending his hand. I smiled, shook hands and then he turned and said, "I think you should marry this girl, Bill, because you're not going to get much better than this in Greenwich"

I immediately liked Winslow.

"How long have you two known each other?" he asked.

"I just met her tonight. She walked in and sat down next to me."

With this discovery, and obviously trying to direct my attention away from Bill, Winslow turned to me and said, "By the way, I'm Bill's parole officer. He just got out of the slammer for dealing crack."

We all laughed hysterically at that one and the three of us had a great time joking around for the entire evening. The drinks were flowing and we were all feeling no pain.

Winslow decided to call it a night and invited us to come down to the Belle Haven Yacht Club sometime next week. "We'll take the boat over to The Five Mile Grille in Rowayton for dinner," he said to Bill. I was very impressed. Belle Haven is an exclusive area of Greenwich, with many of the estates overlooking the Long Island Sound belonging to celebrities. Bill then asked me if I was interested. Of course, I was.

"Sounds like a great idea, Winslow, I'll give you a call on Thursday to firm things up."

Bill and I decided to stay a little longer. Before we knew it we wound up closing the place. The glaring bright lights were turned on, and Jigs shouted, "All right everybody, it's time to go home."

Bill walked me out to my car. "Let's sit in the car for a while," he said. We slipped into the backseat and, we immediately attached ourselves to each other. He not only looked good, he was a natural at the art of kissing.

"God, I'm thirsty. You live right around the corner. Do you think it would be okay if I came over for a glass of water before I take off?"

The old glass of water trick, I thought to myself. "Only if you promise not to give me a hard time. You can only stay for a minute."

I opened the door to my apartment with Bill in tow. "Wow, this is a great apartment. Look at these wood floors and the layout is so spacious," Bill said as he followed me into the kitchen.

"I'm really happy with the move. I needed to get away from the city. I lived there for twelve years," I said as I handed him his glass of ice water.

We wandered into the living room, sat down on the couch and Bill asked, "But wasn't living in the city exciting?"

"Yes, it was great for a while but I think I stayed too long. It became very routine and I just wasn't meeting the right kind of people. Anyway, I'm just so glad I finally moved to Connecticut."

"Me too," he said playing with my hair and nuzzling my neck. I sat back and was really starting to feel the effects of the alcohol. I drank too much. I grabbed his glass of water from the coffee table and took a sip. I sat back feeling a little woozy. Bill began kissing me and within minutes things really started to heat up. His hands were all over me. "Let's go into the bedroom," he said.

I was drowsy. I turned to Bill and said, "No, we have to stop. You promised, only a minute and a glass of water," I said pushing him away and prying myself from under him.

"You're right, I'm sorry." Bill sat up, rubbed his eyes, yawned and said, "I've got to get going."

I walked him to the door, stood up on my "*tipsy*" toes and gave him a kiss. "I had a great time tonight."

"Humm, me too. Let's get together. I'll give you a call."

THE EPITOME OF GREENWICH

I ran into Winslow the following Thursday night at the other Greenwich haunt, The Boxing Cat. The Cat, as they called it, catered to an older crowd, between the ages of thirty-five to fifty, many of them divorcees... Alimony Alley. The place also offered live music packing them in on Thursday and oddly enough Sunday nights. Winslow was seated at the end of the bar, sipping the martini that seems permanently attached to his left hand. He was paying his bill when I spotted him and we bumped into each other as he was headed for the door.

"Hi, Winslow. How are you?"

He looked at me seeming not to recognize me and said, "Refresh my memory, I don't have my glasses on."

"Marianne Thompson. I met you last week at Brett's when I was with Bill Williams."

"Yes! What happened to you guys? I thought we were supposed to take my boat over to the Grille in Rowayton."

"I really wanted to but Bill never called."

"He's a stupid man, you're a beautiful woman. Give me your number and we'll take the boat up to Rowayton for dinner."

I had never dated a man so much older but maybe I should try it. So, I gave him my number.

At ten-thirty the next morning the phone rang. Feeling groggy from the night before I struggled to pick up the phone. "Hello?"

"Hello Marianne. Winslow Barrett here. How are you feeling this morning?"

"Not very perky. Got in late last night."

"Me too. But let's not waste the day. Would you like to go for a boat ride this afternoon?"

"Okay. What time?"

"I'll pick you up at twelve."

I gave Winslow directions to my apartment and dragged myself out of bed. Nothing like a last-minute date but it sounded like it might be an interesting one. Winslow Barrett. This guy seems like the Epitome of Greenwich.

I stepped into the shower and as the hot steamy water cascaded down my back, I felt a little better. My throat was hoarse from all the cigarettes I smoked last night. Overall, I felt like shit. Hungover.

Winslow picked me up in a shiny new Jaguar. Navy blue, tan leather interior, vanity plates with just his initials. WJB. Very classy indeed.

Winslow's hand shook slightly as he turned on the radio and lit a cigarette. He seemed nervous and uncomfortable with himself.

We turned down Field Point Road, and in a few minutes

we entered the very exclusive area of Belle Haven. We drove under an umbrella of towering hundred-year-old oak and pine trees. Rich, dense foliage lined the streets against the neatly manicured lawns of the Great Estates. The view was visually beyond compare.

We passed private roads that had police booths stationed at the entrance, allowing no one to enter who didn't belong. "Diana Ross lives beyond those gates as well as Victor Borge," Winslow pointed out as we drove by.

We traveled down Otter Rock Road and approached the Belle Haven Yacht Club. We circled around the tennis courts, and found a parking spot near the pool house, and then we walked up to the Club House and onto the back lawn. English gardens lined the stone fence that wrapped around the edge of the Long Island Sound. This was the whole nine yards of Greenwich.

"Let's get some drinks to take on the boat. What would you like?" Winslow asked.

"Starting so early in the day?"

"Come on, have a drink. You'll feel better. A hair of the dog that bit you from the night before. A Bloody Mary?" Or how about a Mount Gay Madras? It's the drink of sailor's. Rum, Orange Juice and Cranberry."

"I'll have a Madras."

Minutes later, Winslow returned with the drinks and we headed over to the dock. He flipped the ladder over the edge and we boarded his thirty-foot cabin cruiser. Pretty damn nice. Old Winslow was looking better and better to me. I sat down in the seat next to the captain's chair, leaned back in the soft leather and felt like a million bucks.

"Let's take a spin around the coastline. I'll give you a little tour of the great estates," he said as he started up the engine and slowly pulled away from the dock. As we hugged the coastline, he pointed out the homes of celebrities and prominent people. Winslow was in the real estate business so his knowledge in this area was a little more in-depth. "There's the Trump estate," he said pointing to a huge Mediterranean-style estate. "It's on the market for seven million. And next to it is the home of a woman I used to date in high school, Muffy Blanchard."

The land of Muffy and Biff. This guy's a riot. But I was in awe as we passed these tremendous estates, with rolling green lawns that went on forever until they met with the rocky edge of the Long Island Sound.

"Let's go over to The Atlantis for lunch, you know, the place right in the harbor. I hope there's some docking space available," Winslow said as he lit up another cigarette. He was smoking like a fiend.

"Sounds good to me," I said, leaning back feeling totally relaxed taking in the warm summer sun.

Winslow pulled back on the throttle, and we picked up speed heading in the direction of the restaurant. He then turned to me and said, "I'll tell you how old I am, if you tell me how old you are."

"I'm thirty-nine."

"You're kidding. Geez, you don't look it. I would take you for about twenty-eight! Have you ever been married?"

I hate that question.

"No," I replied feeling a little insecure.

"Wow, how did you manage that? I can't believe it. You have everything going for you. Why didn't you marry?"

I stared out onto the horizon and a feeling of intense sorrow came over me. I never had an answer to that question. I only knew that none of my relationships panned out.

I quickly turned the attention back on him finding out a little more about him.

Winslow was fifty-two and twice divorced. He was also a "T.F.B"...Trust Fund Baby. He came from old money with the source of the money coming from his great, great, great, great grandfather, whose business was similar to mine; the rag business, making all the uniforms and blankets for the North and the South in the Civil War. His family had lived in Greenwich for five generations making him what they call a "townie".

We casually dated for about a year, spending most of the time yacht club hopping and dining out. Winslow dined out six out of seven nights. It was all very exclusive. But the thing that bugged me about Winslow was his teasing me about my New York accent. "Darling," he would say, "You sound like you come from the other side of the Sound," meaning the Long Island Sound. You see Winslow's upper crusty accent was something similar to Locust Valley Lock-jaw, where one must keep the mouth clenched while speaking. He thought everyone should sound like him. "I think it's your elocution. You don't enunciate your words," he would say. Then I would retort, "Who are you Henry Higgins? The rain in Spain falls mainly in the plain." The dynamic duo hits Greenwich.

He made me so paranoid about my accent that I made an appointment with a speech therapist, who told me my accent wasn't that bad. What I needed was a new boyfriend. Culture Clash was the problem, not my accent. He wasn't the guy for me after all. We both had different agendas, with me wanting to get married and pop out a couple of kids, and Winslow just out to have fun. Too much fun. Winslow was an alcoholic.

"Technically, I'm an alcoholic," he told me one day. He wasn't a sloppy drunk and he could carry on an intelligent conversation but he drank everyday. Heavily. And as time went on he became extremely verbally abusive and when it reached an unbearable level, I ended the relationship. I never took our relationship seriously but in the end, it took a toll on my self-esteem. Why was I in this relationship to begin with? There was no future for us. I suppose it was the taste of Greenwich I liked, no matter how sour it was.

I hit the big 4-0 shortly after my relationship with Winslow ended. I was really starting to get depressed about my situation in life. My ovaries were about to blow up and I still hadn't found Mr. Right. Was it ever going to happen? My heart was sinking fast. I couldn't understand why I was in this situation. I was so tired of the singles scene.

I was ready to throw in the towel.

HAIL MARY

The Stamford Town Mall was bustling with throngs of shoppers. As I browsed around the stores, I couldn't decide what to get my cousin Jim for his birthday. I finally picked out a handsome cotton sweater, had it gift wrapped and headed home to get ready for the small, intimate dinner party his new bride, Laura, was giving him tonight. It should be a good party because Jim is always a blast to be around, the quintessential party animal, sometimes getting a little carried away but for the most part just someone who's a lot of fun. Pam, who is Jim's sister, would meet me there.

Jim and Laura started dating about two years ago and within these two years, they got married, went on a fabulous honeymoon and nine months later they had Kyle, a beautiful baby boy. Bada-Bing-Bada-Boom! Now that's the kind of deal I'm after.

I arrived home with just enough time to get ready for the

party. I took a quick shower and started to dress. I put on my last bit of make-up, sprayed my hair and went over to the full-length mirror to take a look at the new casual fit and flare dress I had picked out for the party. Not bad. This dress really made me look slim.

Good Butt Coverage.

I left the house about six o'clock, got in the car and headed north on I-95. Jim and Laura lived in Norwalk, Connecticut about fifteen miles north of Greenwich. They live in a section that's family-oriented, a little more afford-able than Greenwich, and a place I wouldn't mind living in if I ever get married. But at the rate I'm going who knows if that's ever going to happen.

I pulled into the driveway of their new home, picked up the gift from the back seat and walked up the slate walk-way. The house is a classic New England home: a four-bedroom colonial painted white with black shutters and trim. The house looked wonderful and as I walked toward the door, I couldn't help but think how lucky Jim and Laura were and how many nice changes they had gone through in the last year-and-a-half. Maybe I'll pick up some pointers tonight.

Laura opened the door looking great as usual with her classic good looks; blond shoulder-length hair pushed back with a plaid headband, khaki pants, loafers, crew neck sweater---the preppy Ralph Lauren look. Talk about New England overkill.

We gave each other a kiss, a hug, and a big hello and I handed Laura the gift as Jim took my coat and hung it in the hall closet.

"The place looks great, Laura. You did a fabulous job decorating. And where's little Kyle?"

Before I got the words out of my mouth, I heard a giggle in the kitchen, I poked my head in and there he was with Pam. He was so cute with his baldhead. All the babies in our family are bald until they're about two years old; fair-skinned creatures that we are.

"Hi Pam, how ya doing?" I asked, and smiled.

"Good." She then turned the baby toward me, and said, "Say hello to Aunt Marianne, Uncle Fester."

"Uncle Fester," I said with a laugh. "From the Adams Family? Who nicknamed him that?" At this point I was hysterical because he was bald as a bat, had sort of a mature face, and that nickname really seemed to fit.

"Jim named him that."

"You are so funny, Jim."

Laura was finishing setting the table and Pam was helping in the kitchen.

"What would you like to drink?" Jim asked.

"Vodka Cranberry would be great. Thanks."

We took our drinks into the living room. Kyle waddled over, Jim picked him up, turned to me and said, "Having a child is a great experience. Don't you want to have one?"

"Of course I want to have a child, that's my biggest dream. I've tried everything from singles bars, personal ads, dating services. I've dated a ton of guys, but nothing pans out."

Jim took another sip of his drink and said, "Don't worry, it will happen."

"I heard you recently joined a dating service. How did that work out?" Laura asked as she came over to join us in the living room.

"What a nightmare that was. The first guy they introduced me to was a non-smoker and I asked for a smoker.

The second guy lived an hour and a half away, a widower fifteen-years-older than me with three teen-age boys and definitely not interested in having any more children. My third date was a giant, probably 6'7" and in dire need of major dental work. And this agency told me they have an eighty percent success rate, gave me extensive personality tests and was supposed to match me with someone compatible in age, attractiveness and interests. For three introductions the fee was $700, which I haven't paid, the charge is in dispute with American Express and I am trying to get a refund. Another Dating Nightmare," I said, burying my face in my hands.

"Oh God, it sounds horrible," Laura said shaking her head, with a pained look on her face.

Pam popped her head in from the kitchen and said everything was just about ready so we all stood up and walked to the dining room.

The menu consisted of filet mignon, baked potatoes and asparagus with hollandaise sauce. The sauce was delicious. Right to the thighs.

"Laura, you've outdone yourself," I said as I helped Pam clear the table and load the dishwasher. Laura started putting the birthday candles on the cake. We all broke out and sang Happy Birthday to Jim, sat down for cake and coffee.

Laura returned to the table to refill our coffee cups, she then sat down next to me and said, "I think you should pray for a husband."

"You've got to be kidding."

"No, I'm not. You should say a novena. It really works."

"She's not kidding, it works," Jim chimed in, nodding his head in agreement.

They're sounding a little weird, I thought. I remember

Pam telling me how religious Laura was and how Jim kind of jumped on the bandwagon, but this was really out of character for the quintessential party animal.

"Laura, I'm not really religious. I believe in God, don't really believe in organized religion, but I go to Church on Easter and Christmas and that's about as far as I go."

"What do you have to lose? Nothing else seems to be working. Just say the rosary every day for 60 days. It takes about 20 minutes. You remember how to do it, 10 Hail Mary's, one Our Father, a Glory Be to The Father and you say that ten times."

"Laura, really I don't think that's for me. Besides I don't have any rosary beads," I said trying to get out of this as gracefully as possible.

"Oh, I have some I can give you." And on that note she ran upstairs to get them for me.

"Jim, what's going on? This is a little strange and not at all like you," I said as I put down my coffee cup.

"It really works. We said a novena that I would be able to sell my condo quickly and it sold right away."

"You're not supposed to pray for material things!" I screeched. "That's ridiculous, Jim."

"I know you're not supposed to pray for material things, but it just helps me. I say it everyday."

Okay, I thought to myself, my cousin has turned into a religious freak. Well, I guess things could be worse. A few minutes later, Laura came back downstairs.

"Here you go," she said as she handed me the rosary beads. "Just do it, you have nothing to lose, you're running out of time, if you ever want to have a child."

I felt like she was detonating my ovaries.

"Well, I don't know. I don't think it's for me and I don't

want to talk about this anymore," I said as I slipped the rosary beads in my pocket. My cousins had really gone off the deep end.

We changed the subject, thank God, and went back to our usual joking around, but it started to get late and I thought it was about time I headed home. I kissed everyone good-bye. With Laura reminding me about the rosary as I left, I gave a sigh of relief as I got into my car.

On the way home I couldn't help but think how strange Laura and Jim were acting. I guess I shouldn't get down on them just because they've gotten a little religious in their old age but it was so out of character. A novena for a husband, how ridiculous.

I yawned as I opened the door to my apartment. The party had been fun but I was tired and couldn't wait to get under my warm, cozy, down comforter. I undressed, put the rosary beads on the dresser and dozed off.

The next morning when I awoke, the rosary beads were staring at me. When I went to bed that night they were still staring at me. Annoying little buggers. I had trouble falling sleep that night, which wasn't unusual for me, tossing and turning, my mind racing and my heart feeling lonely and scared. I hated nights like this. They came all too often, for the demons always seem to come out at night. Maybe I should pray for a husband, I thought. What the hell, might as well give it a try since nothing else has worked. I stumbled out of bed making my way toward the dresser and took the rosary beads back to bed with me.

I started to pray and it felt very awkward at first but after a while it was very relaxing. The repetition of the prayers almost became like a meditation, my eyes became very heavy and I found myself getting very sleepy. This was better than Tylenol P.M.

Night after night I prayed and I really decided to make a go of it. Believe it or not, I was saying a novena for a husband. Even Ripley would have a hard time believing this. For sixty nights I had to say the rosary and at times I wondered if I would be able to do it. After a few days I decided to ask God also to help me solve my problems because I figured this would probably help me find a husband.

I couldn't really pinpoint what was wrong with me. I was constantly in and out of depression and at times felt very insecure, but I suppose everybody has moments of insecurity. I also had a lot of free-floating anxiety that created tension in my shoulders and neck. The anxiety followed me everywhere, from the train ride to the office and then right into bed with me at night. I didn't know why I had this anxiety; I just knew it was there, every day. So, every day I prayed and prayed and prayed, Please God, please bring me a husband and help me solve my problems.

THE MAN OF MY DREAMS?

Six weeks went by, I was becoming more and more hopeful that my prayers would soon be answered. I felt more confident, more alive, and was sure my lucky day was right around the corner.

It was Tuesday, a beautiful day in June and I was in a particularly good mood. My day at the office was going well and I felt like going out after work for a bite to eat, so I called Pam and asked her if she would like to go to the Boxing Cat for dinner. She was also in the mood. We made plans for her to pick me up at seven o'clock, just enough time to get home from the train station, freshen up my make-up and dress a little more casually.

We sat down at the bar, ordered two glasses of Chardonnay and asked the bartender if we could look at the menu for dinner. Since neither one of us was that hungry we decided on appetizers and salad. After a few minutes I wanted a cigarette so I got up and headed for the cigarette machine but the damn thing ate my money and I didn't get any cigarettes.

I went over to the nearest bartender and said, "The cigarette machine was hungry and ate my money." The guy sitting next to me having a pizza started to laugh. Then we all started to laugh. The bartender gave me my money back and I went next door to get cigarettes.

When I got back the appetizers were served and I noticed that guy across the bar was looking at me. We smiled. I waved and started to eat.

"Pam, I think that guy at the end of the bar is attractive. He keeps looking at me."

"I don't think he's so hot."

"He seemed nice when I was over there getting my cigarette money back. Don't be such a snob."

After we finished our meal, the bartender came over and said, "The gentleman at the other end of the bar would like to buy you a drink."

"That's very nice. I'll have another Chardonnay." This was to be my third and since I was feeling no pain, I decided to mosey over and thank him personally for the drink.

"Hi, that was very nice of you to buy me a drink."

"It's my pleasure. What's your name?"

"Marianne Thompson. What's yours?"

"Robert Brenner, pleased to meet you," and with that I pulled up a chair and sat down next to him.

He lived in the next town, Stamford, moving to the area a year ago just as I did. Before that he had lived for fifteen years to my twelve on the Upper East Side of Manhattan, his shoebox was only a few blocks away from my shoebox. I sat there shaking my head at the similarities. "We were neighbors and didn't even know it", I said. "So what do you do for a living, Robert?"

"I own a company that is opening up Cable T.V. to 300 channels."

"What's the name of the company?"

"Omega Sound," he replied setting down his wine glass.

"Wow, that sounds interesting. What's it all about?"

"Basically through Omega Sound and Cable TV you'll be able to listen to any CD currently on the market before deciding whether to buy it. Since you'll order over the phone we are able to discount all CDs."

"How did you get into that?"

"I've been in the music industry for years. I was a recording engineer before this."

"Oh, did you ever work with anyone famous?"

"Yeah, I've worked with George Benson, Richie Havens, The Stones."

"Well you certainly have had an interesting career." I said thinking this guy is really special.

"I can't complain. What about yourself? What do you do?"

"I'm a production patternmaker in fashion. Do you know what that is?" I asked leaning back in my chair.

"Yes, I used to go out with a girl whose mother was a production patternmaker."

"Isn't that a coincidence?"

We sat and talked, finding out a little more about each other, as we looked into each other's eyes. I felt myself becoming very attracted to him. He certainly seemed to have a lot going for himself, was a good conversationalist, and nice looking. He looked like Tom Hanks: not very tall, probably about 5'8", with curly brown hair and a warm smile with a slight gap between his front teeth.

"How old are you, Robert?" I asked feeling apprehensive.

"Thirty-four."

"That's a great age," I said with a smile, trying to keep my gracious composure. I hope he doesn't ask me my age, I thought nervously; he's six years younger than me. Well that's not too bad. My last boyfriend was seven years younger, and people usually take me for around thirty, but I had better change the subject.

"Where exactly do you live in Stamford?"

"Strawberry Hill, I'm renting a condo there but, I'm thinking about buying it," he replied.

"Don't buy in Stamford, you should buy somewhere around Wilton, since you don't have to commute. That's a much nicer area."

Robert put his arms around me and said, "Maybe some-day you and I will get married and we will both move to Wil-ton."

"You never know, you just never know," I replied blush-ing, and looking into Robert's eyes hoping that something might materialize out of this magical night. God, he was so charming. I couldn't believe he was joking around about marriage. I knew it really didn't mean anything but, how strange.

"You are so beautiful, Marianne. You have such gor-geous red hair and such a pretty smile."

"Thanks, you seem like a really nice person. I'm glad we met."

Just then Pam started to meander over. She had run into a fellow she was dating and had been talking to him and his friends. Looking a little buzzed, she whispered in my ear, "So, what's with you and this dude?"

I clenched my teeth, turned my head away from Robert, looked directly into Pam's eyes and said sternly, "I think he's very nice and I am enjoying his company."

"Well it's getting late. We should get going soon."

"Alright, just give me a couple of minutes," I said and she wandered back to her friend.

"We've got to get going Robert, it's getting late."

"Can I get your phone number?"

"Sure," I said as I reached over, grabbed a bar napkin and wrote my number. I then looked up, smiled, and said, "Well, it was really nice meeting you, sorry the night has to end so soon." I leaned over, looked in Robert's eyes, and gave him a gentle kiss on the lips, hoping to hear from him soon.

The very next day, I had a message on my machine, "Hi, this is Robert Brenner, I met you at the Boxing Cat last night, please give me a call back at 557-6227.

He called! He called! I'm so excited!, I said to myself as I flipped on the stereo and started dancing to the music. Well, at least we were off to a good start. He called the very next day. That's a good return, I thought, as I dreamily sank into the couch brimming with excitement. I waited about fifteen minutes, composed myself, and then picked up the phone and dialed his number.

"Hello, Robert, this is Marianne."

"Hi! How you doing? I was hoping it was you."

"I had so much fun last night. I'm glad you called. So, where are you? At the office?"

"Yeah, I'm always in the office, that's why I gave you this number, it's much easier to reach me here since I'm usually here until ten o'clock."

"Ten o'clock! That's kind of late isn't it?"

"Well, I'm trying to get this thing off the ground. We'll be testing 300,000 homes in Manhattan starting in July."

"Oh my God, you really do have your work cut out for you."

"Yeah, but, I still have a little time to play. Would you like to get together Friday?"

"Well, Friday I'm going to the Crab Shell with the girls."

"Hey, that's right around the corner from my office, you should stop by."

"That's girls night out. How about Saturday?"

"Saturday we're moving the office to the fifth floor. You should see the space. We're going to have half a floor; it's huge compared to what we have now. So, I'll be working all day and into the night but, we could get together a little later on about nine-thirty for a few drinks and maybe watch the game. The Knicks are in the playoffs tomorrow."

"Sure, we could get together later on in the evening. That would be okay with me."

"Great, I'll give you a call Saturday afternoon."

"Alright, I'll talk to you then. Bye."

I hung up the phone, put my hands behind my head, and dreamily plopped back on the couch. He seems so nice, I thought to myself. I am in Heaven. This is so exciting!

A few minutes later Pam called. "Pam, that guy I met at the Boxing Cat just called, isn't that great?"

"You mean Howdy Doody?" she replied giggling, making fun of the space between his teeth.

I told you she had that sense of humor that made me want to go straight for her jugular. At that very moment, I wanted to kill her.

"Pam, that's not nice! I don't say anything nasty about that guy Ed you're dating."

"Oh, I was only kidding. What do you think of Ed anyway? Do you think he's good looking?

"Not really, as a matter of fact, I think he looks rather effeminate. A little light in the loafers."

"He does not! How could you say that?"

"I was just giving you a shot of your own medicine, Pam. Get it?"

"Alright, let's just forget it. So when are you seeing him again?"

"Saturday night."

"That's nice, I hope you have fun."

A few more minutes of small talk went by and we said good-bye ending the conversation, I suppose, on a civil note. She could be so cruel.

I went to bed that night, thinking about Robert, hoping that maybe this could be the one. I finally fell asleep at 1 o'clock; the anticipation of my first date with him was keeping me up.

The next day work flew by, my spirits were definitely up and, the girls at the office found the news of the new man very exciting. I didn't want to jinx it by talking about it too much but I had to tell Kathy, the designer, the good news. She was such a doll, I knew she would be happy for me.

By four o'clock Saturday afternoon I still hadn't heard from Robert. I was getting very nervous. What if he doesn't call, I thought to myself, not wanting to call him. I don't feel comfortable calling men. Oh, don't worry, I said to myself trying to calm down. He's just real busy. He'll call soon. I lay down on the couch, fluffed the pillow under my head, and closed my eyes, deciding to take a little nap.

At a quarter to six, I heard the phone ringing, rubbed my

eyes and in a very low, sleepy voice, answered, "Hello?"

"Well, I see somebody's taking a little nap," Robert said with a chuckle.

Still in a dreamy state, I answered with a giggle in my raspy voice, "Yes, I just decided to put my head down for a little while."

"Yes! Yes! It's Rita Hayworth," Robert said joking around, but what a compliment.

"So are we on for tonight?"

"Of course, I'm sorry I called you so late, I've just been so busy but I should be finished up around nine o'clock so nine thirty is still good for me. Do you want to go over to the Boxing Cat?"

"Sure, I'll meet you over there, it will be easier for you."

"Don't worry about me, I'll pick you up."

"Don't be silly. God, you've been working all day, there's no reason why you should come all the way to Greenwich and then back track towards Stamford. I'm trying to be nice."

"Well that is nice of you, thanks. So, I'll meet you over there at nine-thirty."

Oh, I'm so glad he called I thought as I jumped up off the couch. Now, I have to find something to wear for my hot date. Let's see, something casual but sexy, I said to myself as I started rifling through my closet. I know, I'll wear my little black mini skirt, black flats; he's not too tall, and my oversized white shirt with the embroidery across the top. It looks good when I grab the shirt tales, tie them, and knot them up front instead of tucking in the blouse. Okay, I'm set with the outfit now I've got to hop in the shower, blow out my hair, put on my make-up and be on my way.

I arrived at the Boxing Cat on time to spot Robert seated

at a cozy, little table for two off the bar area. He waved me over. I smiled and said, "Hi, how are you?"

"A lot better since you're here."

I sat down feeling a little nervous. The waiter came by, took my drink order and handed me a menu. "How did the move go?" I asked.

"Oh man, we were so busy. Had to move everything upstairs, hook up the computers, and get the place as organized as possible. For the most part, we're pretty much set up and ready to go."

The waitress came by, took our order, and we began finding out a little more about each other. He came from a pretty modest background, growing up in a small town in upstate New York near New Paltz. His father was a construction worker, his mother a housewife, and they had both passed away. God, they died so young, leaving only him and his sister.

When I asked Robert if he had ever been married, he looked sad, disappointed and a little embarrassed as he put his head down and said, "No."

"Well, I've never been married either," I said understanding how he seemed to feel.

He was rather unassuming for a guy who had come so far. He seemed to be very bright, had won a scholarship to Julliard School of Music in New York. He was a trumpet player. Put sheet music in front of him and he could read it and play it. I was beginning to think he might have been a genius, very talented going from musician, to recording engineer, to thinking of this Cable TV idea and putting it in motion for the past ten years.

We finished eating, he had dinner but I just had an appetizer since I had eaten a sandwich at five o'clock. As the waitress was clearing off the table, I spotted a table up front in the bar area, a cozy little table in a dark corner, with a clear view of the TV hanging over the bar. The play-offs were on and the rest of the bar area was pretty crowded.

"Robert, look at the table over there. Why don't we grab it so we can watch the game?"

"You are quick, my lady. Let's go."

We ordered coffee to be sent to the table in the main bar area, grabbed our wine glasses and headed up front trying to get there before anyone else spotted my find. Robert put his arm around me and said, "Now let's go back to where we left off the last night I saw you."

He then leaned over and kissed me gently, and again gently, and finally he gave me a long, deep, passionate kiss that had me melting. I was instantly ignited, sexual passion swelling up deep inside me with an excitement I knew would be hard to tame. I was falling for this guy and the chemistry was electrifying.

As we finished our coffee and after dinner drinks we both realized it was getting late. Robert had to get up early and go to work, on Sunday no less, and it was inevitable that this glorious evening would have to end. Robert paid the check, we got up, and he took my hand in his and walked me out to my car.

"I had a great time," he said as he leaned over, put his hands around my waist and pulled me towards him. We were like magnets, lips coming together passionately, long deep kisses, bodies pressing together and our hands running up and down each other's spines. I wanted him so badly.

"Do you like champagne?" he asked. I have some back at my place."

"Yes, but I'm not going back to your place. It's only our first date," I said, gently kissing him, knowing that we were both getting a little too excited. "Besides, you have get up early tomorrow. You work too hard, do you know that?"

"Yeah, I know but it will only be for a little while longer."

"Well, I guess we should call it a night, even though I don't want to," I said, feeling sad that the evening had to end so soon.

I got into my car and as Robert walked away, I couldn't seem to let go of him so I opened the car door, stuck my head out and said with a giggle, "Hey you, don't I get a good-night kiss?" Robert laughed, ran back to the car, and gave me one more long, deep passionate kiss that went right through me, leaving me longing for him even more.

THE OMEGA MAN

A week had gone by and I hadn't heard from Robert, but he told me he was going to Lake Placid the weekend after I met him so I probably shouldn't have been worried. God, he was so busy with that company. It sounded like it was going to be something really big. I had to learn how to take it slowly; I expected so much in the beginning. Once I had a friend who told me for the first three months in a relationship nobody owes anyone anything. Maybe I should take her advice.

I finally did get a message from Robert the following Thursday but by the time I called his office I only got the machine so I left another message. I wondered if I was ever going to see him again. Another weekend had come and gone and I was really getting bummed out.

The following Monday, I met Christine in the city for dinner at El Rio Grande, our favorite Mexican restaurant.

The place has an enormous stuffed buffalo with these huge wings hanging over the bar. A Flying Buffalo --what a sight that is--a taxidermist's delight. Only in New York. It had to be an early night for me since it was Monday although Christine was off the next day. She is a nurse with a crazy schedule.

We sat down at the bar, ordered two frozen Margaritas, no salt, and she listened closely as I told her about the exciting new man in my life with all the particulars of his company.

"Christine, I really like him but I'm a little worried. I met him on Tuesday and he called me on Wednesday. I saw him that Saturday night and he told me he was going up to Lake Placid with his buddies the following weekend. He called me the Thursday after that and left a message. I returned the call but I didn't hear from him the whole weekend. I don't understand it, he seemed so interested and said the nicest things to me," I said with a sigh.

"Marianne, don't worry, you just met him. Give him a chance. He left you a message on Thursday. He must be very busy with his business. Don't worry, he'll call."

The host came up to us about twenty minutes later to say our table was ready. Before we knew it we were stuffing our faces with Chicken Fajitas, and telling each other the latest gossip in our lives. The evening flew by so when I checked my watch it was already nine-thirty and time to get going soon if I was to have a good night's sleep. We paid the check, hugged and kissed each other good-bye with Christine promising to visit me in Greenwich one weekend soon.

I put the key in my door at ten-thirty, immediately got undressed and into bed, just about to fall asleep when a minute later I remembered, holy shit, I have to say the rosary. Wearily I grabbed the rosary beads from my nightstand. I wasn't about to stop here since I had already faithfully said forty-five; I started this thing, I had to finish. Please God, please help me solve my problems and please bring me a husband.

The alarm clock rang and I immediately hit the snooze alarm. I really didn't feel like getting up, but I had a big day ahead, flying off to Dallas, Texas for the Merchandise Review Session with our biggest account, J.C. Penney.

I told you for the most part, the World of Fashion is far from glamorous. Bore, bore, and bore.

We also sold to more upscale retailers such as Lord and Taylor, Macy's, and Nordstrom but were it not for J.C. Penney we wouldn't be in business. Middle America is the backbone for the majority of clothing manufacturers. I believe J.C. Penney's is the second largest retailer in the country with the first, get this, K-Mart.

Pardon me while I get my throw-up bag.

I certainly didn't have dreams of J.C. Penney's and K Mart when I graduated from the Fashion Institute but the majority of manufacturers carry either moderate or low moderate merchandise. That's where the bulk of the business is, and that's where most of the jobs are. Well, at least my company doesn't sell to K-K-K-K---K-Mart. It's hard for me to get the words out.

As I started to dress, I began planning the big day in my head. It was going to be gruesome. I had to catch the six-thirty a.m. flight to Dallas, pick up a rental car, drive forty minutes to J.C. Penney's complex, attend the meeting, and then catch the four-thirty p.m. flight back home that same afternoon. No fun at all. These turnaround trips were just too much for me and I told my boss that this would be the last time I would do it in one day. It was just too exhausting.

Just before I left that morning, I was puttering around in the living room looking for my Dallas guide to dining-- at least I had to find an expensive restaurant to have lunch in----and I looked over at my answering machine and noticed it was blinking. I had forgotten to check my messages last night. I pushed the playback button and to my delight the message was from Robert. My adrenalin surged as I listened to Robert's message telling me he had had a great time and wanting to know if I would like to get together again. As I locked the front door, my spirits were sky high, so much so, I probably didn't need a plane to get me to Dallas.

As I sat in the confinement of my airplane seat, flipping through a magazine and getting restless, I decided to make my flight a little more exciting by calling Robert on the airplane phone. I ran my credit card through the slot on the phone, dialed his office number and nervously waited while the receptionist put me through.

"Hi, Robert, how are you?"

"Hey, what a nice surprise to hear from you so early in the morning."

"I didn't get your message until this morning. I had dinner in the city last night with my girlfriend Christine. How was your weekend?"

"Busy."

"I know you went to Lake Placid but then you left a message on Thursday after you got back and I thought we would get together for the weekend."

"I'm sorry, I've just been so busy. I have so much shit to

do, you can't imagine. The business has been really taxing on me with the move and all. So what have you been up to?"

"Well, I'm on my way to a business meeting in Dallas. I'm calling you from the plane."

"You're calling me from the plane? I can't believe you're calling me from the plane!" Robert sounded so excited; I could feel him jumping out of his seat. He then said, "You are a very impressive young lady! What a thrill."

We continued talking and laughing for a while but the call was getting very expensive. "It was great talking to you again, Robert."

"Are you going to be in the office tomorrow?"

"Unfortunately."

"Well, I'll give you a call tomorrow, and we'll plan on getting together."

"Okay, I'll talk to you tomorrow."

When I arrived home late that evening, I was totally exhausted. The only highlight of the trip was my luncheon at the Mansion at Turtle Creek, the most exclusive restaurant in Dallas. I had to get something out of the deal so I ordered everything from soup to nuts. The bill came to $100. Lunch for one. Can't wait to turn in this expense ticket.

I plodded through the next day at the office with so much jet lag I barely made it to five o'clock. I was waiting for Robert's call, but it never came. He told me he would call me at the today and I was really looking forward to hearing from him since our last conversation on the plane was so exciting. I left the office disappointed but hoped I would hear from him that evening. The evening dragged very slowly as it usually does when waiting for a guy to call. I was really bummed out as I got into bed, wondering if I would hear from him again since so many men have pulled the disappearing act on me. Men always say they're going to call on this day or that day and they usually screw up but they do call eventually.

Sure enough, I heard from Robert the next day, and I was so happy to hear his voice, I didn't mention anything to him about not calling yesterday, I just figured he was busy.

"I'd really like to see you tonight, but I have an important meeting this afternoon in the city with my investment bankers and The Griffin Group."

"The Griffin Group? You mean Merv Griffin?"

"Yes, Merv Griffin, famous entertainer who became an extraordinary entrepreneur. They might be interested in investing in the company."

"Wow, that's great! I'm impressed. What time do you think you'll be done with the meeting?"

"Probably about seven. Maybe we could get together for a late dinner, say somewhere around nine?"

"Sounds great, I'm up for a late dinner."

"Good. I'll pick you up around eight-thirty."

I was in heaven as I hung up the phone. I ran to Kathy 's office and told her the good news. "I'm so excited, Robert called and I'm having dinner with him after he finishes his business meeting with The Griffin Group. Merv Griffin!"

"Oh my God, Marianne, I'm so excited for you, that's wonderful."

I left the office on cloud nine! So thrilled, I couldn't take my usual nap on the train, my mind racing as I went over all the things I had to do. I just happen to have an appointment at six-thirty to have my hair cut. Jack will have to make me look fabulous tonight. I'll wear my black, off the shoulder, flared knit dress, and I should be in pretty good shape for Mr. Robert Brenner when he arrives at my door-step.

I was ready to go at about quarter to eight and decided to sit down and watch a little T.V. while I waited for Robert. Eight-thirty came and went and my date was nowhere to be found. At about a quarter to nine the phone rang.

"Hi, sorry the meeting ran late and I'm just getting out of here now. Do you still want to get together?"

"Sure, it's okay, don't worry about it, I think the restaurant serves until eleven, I'll be okay."

"Great, I'm leaving now, I should be there in about an hour."

Ten o'clock came with no Robert. At ten-thirty my doorbell finally rang and I was relieved. "I'm so sorry, I just couldn't get out of there fast enough and there was an accident on the FDR Drive."

"Don't worry about it," I said as Robert put his arms around my waist, pulled me close and said, "Come here you," and gave me a kiss, and another kiss, and another kiss as we leaned against the wall in my foyer. It felt so good to finally be in Robert's arms.

"You must be starving, and the restaurant stopped serving at ten-thirty. Let me make you something to eat."

"I don't want anything to eat. I just want to kiss you. Come on, humor me." Robert said as he again pulled my body toward him and kissed me again and again and again. I was in Heaven.

After about ten minutes of kissing I asked, "Would you like to come in? Come on; let's stop for a minute. Sit down, and relax while I make us some drinks."

I made two Sea Breezes and came back to the couch where Robert was sitting. "Cheers! Here's to your arrival at last."

Robert laughed, sat back and with a grin and a look of total satisfaction, said "Boy, what a day."

"Oh, how'd the meeting go with The Griffin Group?"

"Great. We cut a deal. I can't believe I'm doing business with Merv Griffin. Merv Griffin is backing Omega Sound."

"Wow! Congratulations. That's wonderful. Hey, wasn't there a Saturday Night Live joke about Merv?"

"OooooooooooooooMervvvvvvvv."

"Yeah, that was it," I said with a laugh.

Robert then put his arms around me and said, "I've been working on this for ten years! Ten years and ten zillion dollars later, it's finally becoming a reality."

"That's great. You thought of the idea for the company and put together a deal worth millions.

"I did."

"I am so impressed."

"Yes, the man has a brain."

"Why--Why--Why-- You're THE OMEGA MAN!"

"Here I've come to save the Day!" Robert started singing the Mighty Mouse theme song and with that we both sat back laughing. Then Robert slid his arm around my waist, pulled me closer giving me a deep passionate kiss. As soon as he started kissing me, I became very excited. Things were moving too quickly, but it was so hard to control ourselves. Robert pulled the top of my dress off my shoulder, lowered his head and gently kissed me. I wanted him so badly. It took all the energy I had to say, "Robert, please, we're getting out of hand. We have to slow down."

Robert sat back as I pulled the top of my dress back up around my shoulders where it belonged. "You're just so beautiful," he said to me. "You're hard to resist."

"I think you're wonderful," I said as I snuggled up and he put his arm around me. "Let me make us something to eat and refresh our drinks.

"I just want you," he said, gently kissing me. It was starting all over again. Our lips pressing together, mouths parting, deep passionate kissing and then Robert stopped. He leaned back on the couch, smiled, and said to me, "Now my life is complete."

RICHTER SCALE COINCIDENCE

The phone rang as I opened the front door. I dropped my bag on the floor and ran to the answer it.

"Hello?"

"Well, hello my love. You sound a little out of breath."

"Hi Robert! I just walked in the door and I rushed to answer the phone. I wouldn't want to miss any important calls." I smiled as I sat down.

"I had a great time last night, and I'd love to see you again tomorrow. I know it's short notice but what do you think?"

"My friend Beth is coming to visit tomorrow from the city. How about Saturday night?"

"I can't, my uncle and sister are coming down to see the place."

This will be the third weekend that's screwed up. I am totally disappointed. Well, I haven't really known him that long, I thought, better not to push it. "Well, why don't you meet me and the girls on Friday night? I think we're going to the Boxing Cat. You'll be surrounded by a bevy of beauties."

"One beauty is enough for me, I guess I'll have to wait until next week to see my love. If that's okay with you."

"Sure, next week would be fine with me. I can't wait, my sweet man."

"Alright my love, I'll give you a buzz at the beginning of the week." I hung up the phone, closed my eyes, and thought to myself, I am crazy about this guy, he is so wonderful, he says the nicest things, Oh my God, I am so happy.

Robert called a few days later and we made dinner plans. He arrived at seven-thirty on Thursday, we had a drink at my place first since the reservations were for eight-fifteen and we had some time to kill. "Let's smooch," Robert said, as he pulled me closer.

"Sounds good to me," I said and, of course, we started to smooch and smooch and smooch. Good thing we had dinner reservations, that was our smooch alarm, otherwise we would never have gotten off that couch.

The restaurant we had chosen was Vallbella, a beautiful, very elegant Italian restaurant that is often frequented by the celebrities in the area. There was a little wait for a table so we went into the bar. We sat down, ordered a drink and I asked the bartender what celebrities frequented the place. He told us Michael Bolton, a regular, was always served compliments of the house since his presence in the restaurant seems to help business.

After about fifteen minutes, we were seated. The waiter

handed us our menus and took our drink order. We were both pretty buzzed and probably didn't need anymore but ordered another drink anyway. Robert turned to me and said as he grabbed my hand, "You are so beautiful. How old are you?" Oh God, he's asking me that question. He's only thirty-four. What am I going to tell him? Better think quickly.

"How old am I?"

"Yes, how old are you?"

I turned to Robert and with a smile said, "Well, I'm the same age as Kim Bassinger and Christie Brinkley."

Robert chuckled and said, "And how old is that, twenty-five?"

"No, I'm forty and fabulous." Might as well act as if my age doesn't bother me.

"You're forty? I'm forty!"

"You're forty! You told me you were thirty-four!"

"I know, I lied, I thought you were twenty-five." We both laughed. I was in shock as I sat there shaking my head.

"I can't believe you're forty and you lied to me."

"Well, I'm sorry. So, you're forty and never been married?" he asked.

"You should talk, you've never been married either."

"No, but there were two times that I was going to get married. Once when I was seventeen to Brenda, the girl whose mother was a patternmaker, and the other time to Stacy, the fashion designer, but she had a nervous breakdown and wanted to kill herself. I just couldn't marry her."

"I know exactly where that girl was coming from! Fashion is a horrendous business. I had a nervous breakdown too, but since that time I decided that nobody was ever going to get me that depressed again." I couldn't believe I was being so candid with Robert. Well, that's one skeleton that flew out of the closet. It seemed so strange that one of the girl's mothers was a patternmaker and the other a fashion designer.

Dinner was served, the meal was delicious, but neither of us hardly touched our plates, we were so enamored with each other, holding hands and just talking away. We ordered coffee and dessert, picking over the fruit tart. The coffee felt good going down because the wine was definitely going to my head. Robert paid the check. Already eleven, we had to get going. We walked out of the restaurant arm in arm. When we got in the car, Robert turned to me and said, "Do you like me?"

"DO I LIKE YOU?" I answered in total shock, emotions just pouring out of me.

"Yeah, do you like me?"

"Do I like you? Why, I love you," I said as I bent down and kissed Robert on the cheek. He looked at me and smiled, and then I felt a little silly. I can't believe I said that so soon, but it just came out.

During the drive home he started talking about the business. "Sometimes doing business is so tough, there are so many vultures out there ready to screw you over."

"You're a Dragon Slayer," I said, with a giggle.

"That's what it's like. It's really difficult, but I guess I could always go back to being a recording engineer."

"Well, it certainly would be a lot easier. Omega Sound is going to be too big. It's going to be so big you're just going to have to give half the money away anyway," I said.

"I haven't even made any money yet and you're already giving it away."

"You know, I saw a biography on Cable T.V. about John

D. Rockefeller, how he was despised by the public because he controlled all the oil in the entire country. Then the anti-trust laws were enacted but that didn't really do much to diminish his wealth because Standard Oil was just broken up into sub-divisions such as Texaco, Sunoco, Mobil and the like. But he had a son, John Jr., who became a philan-thropist and all he did throughout his whole life was to give away the family's money to charitable causes. By doing so he regained the family's reputation and from then on the public looked upon the Rockefeller family in a favorable light."

Robert then turned to me and said, "You're not only beautiful, you're smart." He was so sweet.

We got back to my apartment, Robert parked in front of the building and we started to smooch, touching each other, nibbling on each other's ears, when Robert turned to me and said, "Are you going to hurt me?"

"Oh, I would never hurt you!" I said emphatically, hug-ging him and then putting my head on his shoulder. "I'm infatuated with you, and I'm really excited about us and I think you feel the same way too."

"I DO!" Robert said with such enthusiasm, he just made my heart melt.

"Why don't you come in and stay over."

"No, we should wait, and besides I have a really early day tomorrow."

"I'm sorry," I said buttoning up the top few buttons on my dress. "You're right, I know you have a big day tomor-row."

"That's okay. God, good thing the Greenwich Police weren't on smooch patrol tonight. Now you go in and get a good night's sleep, I'll watch you walk into the building. I'll talk to you soon."

"Okay, my wonderful Dragon Slayer," I said as I leaned over and gave him a gentle kiss good night.

The following night was Friday and Patti, my new friend, and I were going to where else but, Brett's. I had met Patti through my cousin Pam, which was ironic because I have been thinking about ending my relationship with Pam. She was always putting me down with constant digs, I was feeling depressed after I saw her, and I just couldn't take her anymore. Patti was new to the area, around my age, and very nice to me. I was glad to have her company. She also had red hair; we were like sisters.

We arrived at Brett's about nine-thirty, The Tony Archer Band was playing tonight, the crowd was lively and we were set for a fun evening. I began to give Patti the update on Robert and told her I was in Love, Love, Love!

"That's great, when are you going to see him again?"

"He's so busy with the business, I never know when I'm going to see him but I know he'll call me soon."

Later that evening a guy Patti was interested in showed up and they began to gab. I stepped aside to give them some privacy. Minutes later, on my way up to the ladies room Winslow walked through the door.

"Hi Winslow, how are you?"

Winslow gave me a kiss on the cheek and said, "Okay. Can I buy you a drink?"

"Sure, I'll have a spritzer. Be back down in a minute. I'm just going up to the Ladies Room.

Winslow and I had remained friends and we often talked about each other's love interests at the time. So, I gave him the update on The Omega Man and he filled me in on some thirty-year old he was dating. And I thought he was too old for me!

At one-thirty in the morning the house lights went on. "Last call for alcohol," the bartender shouted out. Winslow turned to me and said, "Why don't we go back to my place for a nightcap?"

"Alright, I'll meet you over there."

When I got to Winslow's, he poured us both a drink and I continued talking about Robert. A minute later, I had to go to the bathroom.

I sat down on the pot, and started to think about Robert and how in love I was. When all of a sudden a tremendous fear came over me and I began sobbing uncontrollably.

I could hear Winslow coming down the hall. "Marianne, what's the matter?" Winslow asked with surprise and concern.

"*I'm in Love and I'm So Scared*," I said sobbing uncontrollably. I couldn't stop crying.

He then opened the door and looked at me sitting on the pot, pants around my ankles, face in my hands sobbing and he said, "I've never seen you look more beautiful. Come on, we all go through this at least once in our lives."

He made me laugh but then I said, "Oh my God, I'm soooo *scared*." I wiped my eyes, tried to contain myself and just couldn't understand why this absolute moment of fear came over me. The tears continued, as did the overwhelming feelings of *fear*.

The next day, I did my usual Saturday afternoon chores, lounging around that evening just watching T.V. and vegging out. I hadn't heard from Robert. I was disappointed but I guessed he was probably working. He told me he would be working around the clock trying to get the new office in order; gearing up for the testing of Omega Sound in three hundred thousand homes in New York, and with Merv Griffin's lawyers in town I guess I've been put on the back burner of love.

The following day, I decided that I was going to try a new church, Second Congregational. With all the praying I had been doing, I felt the need to go to church. I was raised Catholic but I didn't get anything out of the Catholic Church finding the services for the most part very boring, and their rules very archaic. This church is a branch of the Protestant religion and I decided to check it out. I had heard its membership is as diverse as the people who live in Greenwich. People from all walks of life, from your average working class residents to CEO's of Fortune 500 companies.

Second Congregational Church, built in the mid-1800, is the prettiest church in Greenwich; a magnificent huge stone structure, set atop a hill that is now covered with the new arrival of spring crocus. The view was breathtaking with a steeple reaching so high up you could see it from the Long Island Sound. It has long been a landmark for sailors since the building is the tallest shore point between New York City and Boston.

I suppose the beauty of the church is what initially attracted me, but looks are very superficial and what I was really hoping to find was a place that would add another dimension to my life; a spiritual one, something that had been missing within me for a long time. There has to be more to life than the well-paying job, the beautifully decorated apartment, the new car, and the boyfriends that come and go. Maybe I could find some answers in the beautiful church that sits upon the hill.

The alarm rang the next morning and I really didn't feel like getting out of bed. Maybe I'll go to church next week, I thought as I rolled over after hitting the snooze alarm. Oh come on get up, I said to myself; there might be something for you at that church. I grumbled a little while longer, rubbed my eyes, and finally decided to get up, shower and get ready for church.

When I pulled into the church parking lot, I was running a little late. I hurried out of the car and walked quickly to the church entrance. The door was locked.

Hmm, this is weird. The parking lot is full, so there must be a service. I guess I have to go around the front.

I decided to walk over to read the glass-enclosed sign posted on the front lawn of the church. When I saw the sign, my jaw dropped, my eyes widened, and I was in utter shock! The sermon, given by Minister Tom Murphy, was entitled... *"Being Afraid to Love."*

My God. Just the other night I was crying to Winslow about Robert and telling him I was in love and so *scared*. Man, this is spooky, I thought, as I walked around to the front door of the church, only to find that door locked too. What's going on? I walked back to the sign for more information. The service was being held in the Waterman Chapel. Hmm, where was that, I questioned, turning to the other side of the building where I finally found an open door.

I slid into a back pew. The service had already started and the Minister, a very handsome young man in his thirties with a very eloquent speaking voice was about to begin his sermon on *"Being Afraid to Love."* I sat there listening with a fierce intensity, motionless as the sermon began:

"One of last year's Academy Award nominations for Best Picture was the film "Remains of the Day" starring Anthony Hopkins and Emma Thompson. Hopkins plays Mr. Stevens, the head butler at a large estate in England. Emma Thompson plays the role of Miss Kenton, the estate housekeeper. The movie is set in the year's immediately preceding and succeeding World War ll.

Mr. Stevens is the central character in the film. His life and work are laid out for the viewer in meticulous detail. In this world, Stevens is a man of absolute dependability. He runs the large estate like a well-oiled machine. Service is the only role he has ever known. Mr. Stevens is a creation of his environment; his position in life has dictated his emotions, feelings and responses.

Enter the beautiful, headstrong, independent Miss Kenton, who is clearly Mr. Steven's equal in relation to her work. Her work is important to her. The difference being that for Miss Kenton, life is a passion. All aspects of life are a part of that passion. She engages, digs deeply and seems to have genuine heartfelt responses to situations and people around her.

The movie was billed as a romance, and it might seem obvious where this story will take us. Two people come together as complete opposites. Each transforms the other and slowly the couple falls in love and lives happily ever after. Correct? Not exactly. You see, contrary to the authority of the Harlequin Romance, it is possible that love will not conquer all, that people can and do choose to keep love away from their lives. If the story was a romance, it was a tragic romance, because love never did get a chance. Mr. Stevens could not accept the possibility of love in his life, because for him, human love is not predictable, it does not conform to any tested standards; and most of all because love challenges us to be revealed "as we are" in the presence of another.

Today, I would like to reflect on love for a few moments. I would like to reflect on the love in our lives that never gets a chance to come to fruition because we are afraid. Now this might be romantic love that we have pushed away, or it may be the love that comes from a very different place; a love that God places in our lives for a reason, be it love of friend, love of neighbor, or love of stranger. There are some kinds of love that we never give a chance, the kind we choose to turn away from in fear and ignorance.

In romantic love there is a supreme joy, and also a supreme fear in connecting to someone in this way. We want to reach out, we want to come closer and yet where will this journey take us? How can we risk when we don't know if we will be safe? Do I love or do I build a wall? Do I speak or do I remain silent?"

I sat there transfixed, emotionally shaken trying to fight back the tears as I listened to him speak. This is such a strange coincidence and what about this sermon; what does this mean? Afraid to Love--I hope that's not Robert. I hope that's not me. Maybe it is me I thought with lips trembling, tears welling up inside me. The service ended and the Minister headed down the aisle, opened the doors of the chapel, and the congregation lined up to shake his hand and say good-bye. As I approached the Minister, the tears began to slowly trickle down my cheeks, and I said, "Thank you so much."

"You're welcome," he replied, looking at me with concerned eyes, but before he could say anything more, I quickly left the church.

As soon as my face hit the fresh air, I burst into tears, running to the car. Oh my God, that was so weird. What

A bizarre coincidence but what does this all mean?

I started the car, looked in the rearview mirror, wiped my tears away, freshened my make-up, and pondered what I had just heard. I couldn't help but think there was a message for me in that sermon.

BURGER, FRIES AND A COINCIDENCE SHAKE

The very next day I decided to invite Robert over for dinner to find out why my weekends kept getting screwed up. I called his office. He wasn't in, so I left a message. The day had passed and I hadn't heard from him. The night had also passed and still I hadn't heard from Robert. Figuring he was busy, I didn't worry about it. But when I still hadn't heard from him the following morning, I was worried; so worried, it ruined my morning and I was really pissed off as I left the office at lunchtime. For some strange reason, I wanted to go to McDonald's for lunch, a choice my stomach would surely regret by late afternoon.

I was angry, upset and worried as I headed up Seventh Avenue towards the Golden Arches. The thoughts that repeatedly ruminated through my mind had only one theme: He's *forty, single, never been married* and the chances of him ever getting married are only about five percent. What about you, I thought, you're forty, single and have also never been married. But, it's different for a guy, they get to do the asking. No, I'm just making a big thing over nothing. This guy is forty, single, and has never been married and he's never going to get married so you had better start looking elsewhere, I said to myself as I opened the door to McDonald's and headed down the aisle for that greasy burger, fries and a dose of indigestion.

I paid for my food, walked upstairs to the smoking section, and since it was so crowded, I sat down and shared a table with a young, attractive black woman. I started to eat as she sat across from me reading *Newsday*. Now, I normally get *Newsday* every day but today I was running late so I picked up the *Daily News* on the train platform instead. I sat and ate, peeking over at her paper when all of a sudden she turned the page to an article entitled, *The Late Blooming Groom*. My eyes widened, my voice went up a few octaves and almost with a stammer, I said, "Is that today's *Newsday*?"

"Why yes, is there something you would like to read?"

"That article you're reading, *The Late Blooming Groom*. This is so strange because I'm dating a guy that's forty, single and never been married, and I kept thinking about that as I was walking over here."

"You can get married at any age. What difference does it make? You can get married at fifty. I'll let you have the paper after I'm finished, I just want to read my horoscope."

I'm totally freaked out. This is really weird I thought. I can't believe this.

After a few minutes, this very nice woman got up, handed me the paper, smiled, and said, "Well, I guess the next time I see you, you'll be married."

Totally taken aback, I smiled nervously, thanked her and quickly turned to the article. I sat there in a state of shock, and began to read.

We've all heard the old wives tale: A man who hasn't married by age 40 is probably a poor bet. Mary Batten, author of "Sexual Strategies: How Females Choose Their Mates", recalls: When I was in college growing up, if a man hadn't married by the age of forty, you had to suspect either he was gay or he had such a strong attachment to his mother that neither you nor he would ever be able to break it.

Well, Robert's mother is dead, and he's definitely not gay, so I don't have to worry about that, I thought, as I read on....

"I think you would know if they were gay," says Vicki Flick, 26, single and a publicity manager for the Putnam Publishing Group. "I think the primary concern is that they just aren't the type of man that can make a commitment and just slip from one woman to another."

I hope that's not Robert, I thought as I continued...

David Buss, author of "The Evolution of Desire: Strategies of Human Mating", suggests there are men whose need for casual sex is so important they are a bad risk for women with marriage in mind. Such men are pursuing a "short-term mating strategy," says Buss, a professor of psychology at the University of Michigan, who has studied the mating preferences of 10,000 people in 33 cultures. "Men into a lot of casual sex sometimes don't want to get married because it restricts the opportunity for casual sex," he says. Of course, they won't admit it openly, he says. "They feign love, feign commitment, and exaggerate the depth of their feelings. Basically, they tell women what they want to hear."

That's definitely not Robert, he's too nice to be someone like that.

Buss suggests women have developed defenses against

such men, for example, being especially sensitive to clues about the "actual depth" of a man's feelings. That's why women talk about their relationships with other women friends, going over conversations again and again. What did he say? How did he look when he said it? "Men never do that, never dissect conversations," says Buss.

Robert seems so sincere when he says those nice things to me....

But, says Buss, there are also men who aren't deliberately jumping from one short relationship to another but are simply "waiting until they meet an unusually special woman."

Ahh, that sounds more like Robert...

I think women should always be open to that exceptional possibility," says Mary Batten, recalling a man she knows, "a wonderful human being," who was 50 when he was first married, to a divorced woman with grown children. "There may be men out there who are highly selective. Let's face it. It's easy to find mates if you don't have particularly high standards, very, very easy."

Still, on the face of it, some experts say, the fact that a man or a woman, hasn't married by a certain age may be a sign that for them marriage has a low priority.

And if the message isn't clear? Mattes, who is also a psychotherapist in private practice in Manhattan, suggests asking yourself a few key questions that speak to the other person's willingness or capacity for a committed relationship. Is this person dependable, for example, following through on promises to get together or call?

Well, sometimes Robert says I'll call you tomorrow and he doesn't. But, he usually calls a day or two later. He's just too busy. Look at the business he has, and it's all just getting off the ground...

Jane Mattes suggests that women ask themselves a few questions if they hope to develop a committed relationship with a man over 40 who's never been married: What happened in his previous relationships, for example? Look for an ability to take responsibility for his part in the breakup, suggests Mattes. And be wary of men who make blanket dismissals of women and their ways.

How involved is he with his mother? "You want them to like their mothers, but not too much," she says. "They shouldn't hate their mothers, but they shouldn't drop everything and have their life revolve around their mothers."

Is he dependable and responsible? "Do they mean what they say and say what they mean?" asks Mattes. "If they say they'll call, do they call?"

Does he seem to be able to negotiate with you? Is there give and take?

How openly does he communicate with you? If he were late for dinner, for example, or said he'd call and didn't, does he take responsibility, apologize and communicate it?

If he repeatedly lets you down by not calling on time or being late or whatever, is it a bad habit he exhibits with everyone or is it something that has to do with his ability to be with you? If it doesn't only apply to you, says Mattes, "You have to decide what your tolerance is for their little quirks as, hopefully, they will tolerate yours."

Wow, how weird is this. I've been *Zapped!* This is freaky, I thought to myself as I slowly, rose from my chair shaking my head, in utter amazement.

I picked up the paper and headed back to the office. I had to get back for a fitting at one-thirty that would be showcasing the new fall line. I walked at a lively pace, dodg-

ing in and out of the hordes of people on the street at
lunchtime, passed by the congregation of patternmakers in
front of 530 Seventh Avenue. It's so funny how everyday
after they eat lunch, a group of about twenty-five patternmakers stand in front of that building, gossiping about the
goings on in the industry. All of them are Italian, short and
male.

Someone should call a sociologist.

When I first entered the business, ninety percent of the
patternmakers were male. Needless to say, it wasn't an easy
climb for this very feminine redhead with the Irish mug, but
I made it.

Anyway, I got back to the office and immediately headed
for Kathy's office. She and the petite fit model, Donna, were
waiting for me. Donna, like most of the models in the industry, worked on a freelance basis and was booked once a
week for an hour. I put my pocketbook down and said,
"Kathy, you'll never guess what happened to me at lunch." I
began telling the girls about the bizarre coincidence, put the
paper on the desk and opened it up to the article.

"Oh my God," Kathy said, opening her mouth in astonishment, cupping her face in her hands. "What does it say?"

Donna and Kathy came closer as I told them, "Well it
says a lot of things. It asks, "does he have a strong attachment to his mother."

"How is Robert with his mother?" Kathy asked.

"His mother is dead."

"Oh, that's good."

We both giggled and I continued skimming and reading
parts of the article. "It also says some men are into a lot of
casual sex and exaggerate the depth of their feelings just to
tell women what they want to hear. But that's not Robert;

he's too nice for that, besides he's got a little nerd in him. It also says some men are simply waiting until they meet an unusually special woman. Oh, that must be it."

"Yeah, I'm sure everything will work out for you." Kathy replied.

"But what a strange coincidence and, the other day I had another really weird coincidence. I went to this church for the first time. Two nights prior, I had been crying uncontrollably; I'm in love and I'm sooo scared. I just had a tremendous fear come over me. Anyway, I go to this church and the sermon is on, *Being Afraid to Love.*

Donna then grabbed my arm and in a voice filled with alarm said, "IT'S NOT A COINCIDENCE!!!" Read this book, *The Celestine Prophecy,* I have it right here in my pocketbook. It's about the concept of meaningful coincidence."

As she pulled the book out of her pocketbook, I jumped back in astonishment, "You're spooking me," I cried out. "What is the book about?" I asked.

"It's about a true spiritual philosophy that is put in story form. Just buy the book and read it." I grabbed a pen and jotted down the title and the author's name.

We then started the fitting with Donna putting on a two-piece suit my samplehand Maria had just finished this morning. The suit looked pretty good needing just minor corrections in adjusting the length of the skirt and opening up the neck a little. I wrote down all the corrections I had to make on the garment, said my good-byes and told her I would buy the book today after work. I walked into my room and on my telephone someone had placed a Post-It message: While you were out, Robert Brenner called at 1:15.

"I'm so happy! He called, he called!" I said to Ida, my fellow patternmaker in the room. I picked up the phone and dialed his office number.

"Hi! How are you Robert? How was your weekend?

"Bizarre."

"Why, what happened?"

"An old college buddy dropped by unexpectedly. It was really a surprise so I hung out with him and his wife on Saturday."

"Oh," I said and at the same time thinking it would have been nice to hang out with them, but I haven't really known him that long. Maybe he felt more comfortable being alone with them since he has known them for so many years. "Well, since you took me out to such a nice dinner the other night, I'd like to ask you over for dinner tomorrow night."

"I'm so busy, I have the lawyers coming in next week to finalize the deal and I have a lot to prepare for but, if I get all my work done, I'll come over."

"That would be great. Give me a call tomorrow and let me know whether or not you can make it."

"Okay my love. If I come over, can we smooch?"

"But of course," I answered in a French accent reminiscent of Inspector Clouseau from The Pink Panther.

"You're a real beauty. Do you know that?"

"Yeah." I said with a giggle.

"Okay my love, I'll call you tomorrow."

The day finished uneventfully and as I cleaned my table off before leaving for the day, I remembered I had to pick up that book Donna told me about. I said my goodnights and headed for Grand Central. I made a quick stop at the bookstore in the station, and boarded the 5:32. I grabbed a window seat for the ride home and began to read the jacket cover. The book is described as a parable filled with vital

truths that contains nine insights the human race is predicted to grasp as we enter an era of true spiritual awareness. The first insight pertains to mysterious coincidences—
sudden, synchronistic events that, once interpreted, lead us
to our true destiny.

I began to read the first chapter and was awe-struck as
it went on to explain: *These coincidences are happening
more and more frequently and that, when they do, they
strike us as beyond what would be expected by pure chance.
They feel destined, as though our lives have been guided by
some unexplained force. The experience induces a feeling of
mystery and excitement and, as a result, we feel more alive.*

*We are experiencing these mysterious coincidences, and
even though we don't understand them yet, we know they
are real. We are sensing, that there is another side of life that
we have yet to discover, some other process operating behind
the scenes.*

*Individuals have been aware of these unexplained coin-
cidences throughout history and this has been the perception
behind many great attempts at philosophy and religion.*

This is really creepy, I thought. This seems to be happening to me right now with those two strange coincidences
and even this book and how I came to it is a strange coincidence.

The book then went on to say that these coincidences
occur when you connect to your *Higher Power*.

Shaking my head, I thought, Oh my God, something is
happening to me.

WHEN A MAN LOVES A WOMAN

Robert called the next day but told me he still had a lot of work to get done and he didn't know if he was going to be able to come over for dinner. I told him that even if he finished the work around nine, he could still come over for a late dinner. He told me he would try to get it done. When I got home, I immediately picked up the phone to call him. I was dying to see him. "So how are we doing with the work schedule?" I asked.

"I'm still not done, and you don't know how much I want to see you."

"Well, I have the perfect solution to our problem."

"What's that?" he asked eagerly.

"I'll bring the food to you. I'll just make some light sandwiches and we could eat at the office."

"Oh, you don't have to go through all that trouble."

"But, I really want to. Besides, then I would get to see the place."

"Well, who am I to say no. Come Woman! Come to the

Fortress of Love." he said, in a lowered voice with his Medieval Knight accent.

I laughed and said, "I will come to meet my Dragon Slayer. I'll be there around seven-thirty."

"Okay, my love. I'll be here."

I hung up the phone and immediately went into high gear. I ran over to the supermarket to get some fresh turkey for sandwiches and some shrimp. Then, at the liquor store, bought a bottle of Kendall Jackson Chardonnay. Only the best for my love.

Ran home, cooked the shrimp; thank God they only take five minutes, made the sandwiches, took a quick shower, put on my make-up, ironed my shirt, and was totally exhausted as I headed out the door with dinner. I relaxed for a while on the ride to his office, which was only ten minutes away.

The Marriott Center was impressive with the glistening glass office buildings one of which was occupied by the love of my life. I was nervous and excited as I parked the car and headed for building 100. I entered a very plush lobby, told the concierge I was here to see Robert Brenner of Omega Sound and he directed me to the elevators. I slid into the wood paneled elevator, pushed the button for the fifth floor, got off and knocked on the door of Omega Sound. I didn't get an immediate response so I tried the door. It was open, so I walked in.

Robert, are you here?"

"I'm back here."

As I followed the sound of his voice, I was amazed at how huge the place was, very plush with all the equipment and furniture being brand new and state-of-the-art. I saw Robert coming toward me with a big smile and I raised the gift-wrapped bottle of wine and said, "Your Fantasy Girl is here!" He gave me a big smile, took the bottle of wine from my hands, set it down on his desk. He then put his arms around me, drew me close to him and gave me a kiss that instantly aroused me.

"Oh, you feel so good," I said dreamily to Robert.

"Umm, you too," he replied while running his hand up and down my back and cupping my backside. "Let me show you around the place. I'll give you the grand tour," Robert said, taking my hand and leading me into the next room

"My God, you really have been busy, how do you do it?"

"One step at a time and things get done."

"Now this is our conference room," he said, pointing to a glass enclosed room, with a huge long table surrounded by twelve very plush red chairs.

"This is beautiful, and the artwork on the walls is fabulous," I said looking over at an exquisite framed photograph that was really a piece of art.

"Yeah, that photograph was taken by a buddy of mine. He's been in a few galleries."

"They're beautiful," I said.

"So are you," Robert said, nuzzling my neck and then gently kissing my lips. Once again taking my hand he led me into the next area. "This is our accounting department, my operations manager's office is over there, and there are a couple of more conference rooms back here, some additional offices over there, and here we are back in my office."

"I am really impressed. This place is beautiful. Look at this handsome mahogany desk you have."

"And, I'd like to have you right on this desk, my love," Robert said, with a chuckle as he kissed my neck and ran his hands up and down my back, bringing them forward and cupping my breasts.

"Oh, that feels so good."

Robert gently unbuttoned my blouse and pushed back my bra, and began bringing me to heights so great I knew I was at the point of no return. "Let's sit down," I said in a dreamy state. Robert eased back onto his huge, oversized black leather executive's chair. I sat on his lap and continued kissing, caressing and touching. He was excited and I could not control myself this time.

I wanted him so badly. The chemistry was so intense. Robert ran his hand up and down my leg and gently slipped off my panties. His hand began stroking me gently, softly, the excitement building. It was complete ecstasy. "Oh, that feels so good," I cried out as I lost control with a feeling I had never known before. Turning to Robert, kissing him deeply, feeling more satisfied than ever before, I now wanted him to have pleasure.

I couldn't contain myself any longer. "Now it's your turn," I said as I began kissing, and touching him until finally I was ready to ravage him. "You're incredible. You're so incredible," Robert moaned and at that very moment I knew he was in ecstasy. "I can't take it anymore." I continued giving myself to him until he finally let out a breath of pleasure. "That was so wonderful," Robert said as he laid back gently breathing out. He gently, pulled me up bringing my lips to his, softly kissing me and nuzzling my neck as I lay my head on his shoulder. We sat back for a few minutes in utter contentment.

"That was wonderful," I said nibbling on Robert's neck. "It certainly was," he said as he kissed my forehead.

We sat there for about five minutes more just cuddling, caressing and slowing down. "Well, are we ready for a glass of wine?" he asked.

"But, of course, my Darling," I said in my French accent.

"You're something else. Come on, let's have it in the conference room."

We made our way out to the conference room, he opened the bottle of wine and when I brought out the shrimp cocktails he said, "This is so nice, this is great." We sat there in utter bliss, talking, sipping our wine, and feeding each other shrimp. After we finished the last shrimp, Robert said, "What do you want to do now? We could go out to dinner if you'd like. I finished most of my work sooner than I thought."

"But I brought turkey sandwiches."

"You are unbelievable. This is great," Robert said as he took the turkey sandwiches out.

"I made them with lettuce, mayonnaise, with a little bit of salt. I hope that's okay."

"Perfect. It's delicious," he said as we began chowing down the sandwiches.

We finished eating, Robert poured us each another glass of wine and we sat back, holding hands when I asked him, "So what's going on this weekend?"

"I have two business plans I have to finish for my investment bankers and it's probably going to take me all weekend. They're about fifty pages each."

I began to seethe and with eyes peering at him said, "You know, you owe me a weekend!"

Robert took my hand in his, looked deep into my eyes and said, "Marianne, I'm going to owe you a lot more than a weekend. I've been working on this for ten years and it's finally coming to a head. This is like going to the Super Bowl and it has to be right. We are going to have our weekends but, for the time being, I have to remain focused on the business. You're an incredible woman and it doesn't get much better than this." Then he lifted his head up, looked at the ceiling and said "Thank you Lord."

"I can wait. I think you're wonderful," I said leaning closer and resting my head on his shoulder.

"No I'm not."

"Well, I think you are." I said feeling so happy just to have him near for this short while.

It was getting late. We both had to work tomorrow, so we reluctantly cleaned up, locked up and headed to the parking lot. Robert kissed me good-bye, thanked me for all the goodies I had brought up to the office and told me he would call me tomorrow.

On my way home I was still in a dreamy state. My God, he says the nicest things to me, more so than anybody I've ever dated. He's just so busy with that business, I suppose he'll fit me in when he can for the time being but, eventually things will settle down. He told me it would take about three months to finalize the deal and I'm going to give him those three months. I've known him for six weeks so far, what's another six weeks. I'll just keep busy. God, I've really fallen head over heels for this guy. I am in Love, Love, Love.

The weekend arrived and I was reminded that Robert would be busy with those business plans he had to get together for Merv, Merv, Merv. I hated the waiting. I know he'll come back as soon as those damn lawyers get out of town but I'm getting tired of all this.

I looked out my kitchen window as I made myself a little lunch and noticed it was a dreary day, the sky covered with clouds with a prediction of rain. Maybe I'll go to the movies today. I sat down to eat my tuna sandwich, grabbed the paper and turned to the movie timetable. I really want to see the movie *When a Man Loves a Woman* but wondered how I would react since it was a movie about a man who is married to an alcoholic and my mother was an alcoholic.

Last weekend I went home to visit my dad, we decided to take a day trip to Southampton, Long Island, and as we were sitting having lunch at the local restaurant, The Drivers Seat, I asked him if he had seen the movie *When a Man Loves a Woman* and he said he had seen the movie but had found it boring. *"Boring?"* I asked, "How could you find it boring? That was your life, Daddy."

"I know," he said looking kind of sad and then just put his head down and continued eating.

I was surprised he even admitted that. He is in denial about my mother's alcoholism. He'll often say, "Your mother was only an alcoholic the last few years of her life. She drank because of her arthritis." This really makes me angry.

But his denial came late in life. When I was younger, he was always making blatant statements about her drinking. I remember once we were shopping in an electronics store and they had on display a "Home Breathalyzer" to test blood alcohol level. He picked it up, looked at it and said, "This thing would blow up if your mother used it." I couldn't help but laugh. As sick as it was the comic relief seemed to help.

We finished our lunch and while having coffee, he began to reminisce, talking about his life, and his work. He was a newspaperman in his day, an advertising salesman, working at different times for *The Journal American*, *The Daily News*, and *The New York Post*. He began telling me that he traveled from 1960-1965 every spring through the summer going up to New England to sell resort advertising, leaving on Sunday night and not returning until Friday night.

As he reminisced, my blood began to boil, the anger and hurt were building up inside me. "Wait a minute, Daddy. You told me you only went away for one summer! And now you're telling me it was for five years! Why did you lie to me? Do you know how traumatic that was for me? I hated it when you went away on business."

"I didn't have a choice, that was my job."

I shot him a look, stabbed a French fry with my fork and went back to eating. After we finished lunch, it was time to go back home to Levittown. Levittown, Long Island, a far cry from Greenwich, Connecticut. There weren't too many blue bloods in Levittown. As a matter of fact, I don't think there were any unless they lost all their money in the stock market. Levittown is strictly middle of the road, but also famous in its own way.

The year was 1945. Bill Levitt built a town for the veterans returning from World War II. Rows and rows of homes all put up within a few short years. Seventeen thousand homes in all, with only a choice of two styles, a ranch or a cape. If you had a hundred dollars to put down, you got yourself a house with a purchase price of eight thousand dollars. So, in one fell swoop, Bill Levitt created a community sprung out of the potato farmland of Long Island, and at the same time coined the term tract housing.

A lot of people, including myself, put Levittown down but it really was a pretty good place to grow up in the fifties. Just think of the concept. All the young veterans and their new brides, all in their twenties and early thirties, all starting families at the same time moving into a brand new town, and within a few short years the neighborhood was clamoring with kids. It was a great era. There were always plenty of kids to play with. Mothers didn't have to haul them off to play dates as they do today. All you had to do was walk out the door and there were a dozen kids. The future baby boomers of America.

Most of the mothers stayed home while the dad's went off to work. They didn't have to hand their newborn babies over to nannies to go to work; it was a one-paycheck family back then. There was a sense of community. When someone new moved into the neighborhood, my mother and her friends would bring food over and welcome them.

A church was built soon after the town sprung up. People went to church every Sunday, dressed in their Sunday best and afterwards the Dunkin' Donuts across the street was packed. Different time, different era. With all the technological advances made in the last fifty years you'd think we would be better off. But are we? We might be more comfortable. That two-pay-check family can buy a lot more. But is it material things that make us happier?

Getting back to the movie, I finished my tuna sandwich and decided maybe I shouldn't go because it might be depressing. As I got up to do the dishes I thought, oh come on, you have to see this movie. I went into the bedroom to get dressed for the day. I pulled on my jeans, grabbed a sweatshirt from the dresser and went into the bathroom to straighten out my hair. I looked into the mirror and decided to go. I laced up my sneakers and out the door I went to catch the one-thirty show.

I paid for my ticket, bought a diet coke and small popcorn, and made my way down the aisle finding a spot center stage. I sat there munching on my popcorn, fidgeting and watching the previews for the coming attractions. Then the movie began and it was my life. The tears streamed down my face as I watched the two little girls in the film watch their drunken mother fall out of the shower, through the sliding glass door and onto the bathroom floor. My mother had once also fallen through the glass shower door.

The father in the movie was an airline pilot, so he was not home at the time, for his job had taken him away from the family. My father was also gone, away on business on many occasions while my mother was falling down drunk. The mother in the movie was always screaming at her children in her drunken, slurred voice, "Do your home- work!"

That was my mother. As she prepared dinner she would be drinking. Scotch. Scotch on the rocks hidden beneath the counter where the dishes were kept, and after she would sneak a long swig on her drink, she would catch us out of the corner of her eye watching her and she would scream out in her drunken voice, "Do your homework!" There were so many similarities in this movie to my life as a child I couldn't help but sit there and cry, throughout the whole movie. The father in the movie would come home in a screaming rage and smash the bottles of liquor in the trashcans outside.

My father smashed them in the kitchen sink.

The only thing that was not similar to my life in the movie was the ending. In the movie the mother goes into a rehab center and quits drinking. My mother never got help. She died an alcoholic and denied ever being one up until her very last day.

PANDORA'S BOX

The following Saturday the girls and I were off to that beautiful little island near the coast of Massachusetts. Beth, Christine and I usually went every year but this year was to be different. Christine couldn't make it so I invited my new friend Patti. And then my cousin Pam wanted to join us.

Pam and I had another blow out last week and I really didn't want her to come, but she kept telling me she didn't want to lose my friendship. Blah, Blah, Blah. Let's make-up. We can have a great time she kept on and on and on so I finally decided it would be the four of us. She had better watch her mouth this time. I'm sick of her insults. The last time we went for a walk around the loop in the park, Pam wanted to jog while I wanted to speed walk. I told her to go ahead and jog, I'll be right behind you but she turned to me and said, "Oh, come on you should jog. You have fat thighs." Did I need this shit? No. Then she told me that since I'm forty I should have a child on my own so that I wouldn't be so lonely. My cousin. I don't think she realizes how she comes off.

I squeezed the last article of clothing into the suitcase, struggled to zip up the bag and sat on the bed totally exhausted. I supposed I over-packed again, as usual. Maybe my entire spring and summer wardrobe would come in handy for our short four-day stay on Martha's Vineyard.

The girls arrived at my apartment at 6:00 a.m.; we packed up the car, stopped at the deli for coffee and were on our way to paradise. We made pretty good time and the trip was actually quite enjoyable as we talked all the way. Even my evil cousin was behaving herself!

We pulled into Woodshole, Massachusetts, just in time to catch the 10:30 ferry to Martha's Vineyard. Forty-five minutes later we stepped off onto the glorious island with it's quaint villages, beautiful clapboard houses with black shutters and neatly manicured English gardens. We drove down the cobblestone streets of Edgartown and checked into the Harborside, a hotel right on the water with breathtaking views overlooking the harbor.

Our first day couldn't have been better. We spent the afternoon at South Beach where the clean, cool, light green surf and pure white sand made for a very relaxing repose compared to the hectic morning. We swam, we laughed, we read, dozed and just completely unwound as the sounds of the surf and the seagulls soaring above gave us the feeling that we were indeed in paradise.

The day soon came to an end. We reluctantly started to pack up and head back to the hotel, but at the same time we were excited about the evening we had planned. Arriving back at the hotel about four-thirty, we showered, dressed and went out to the balcony off our room to watch the sun set upon the harbor. Martha's Vineyard is perfection. We opened a bottle of Chardonnay and toasted our good fortune as we looked out at the beautiful harbor view. We had reservations for dinner at the Shiretown Inn, requesting a table outside in the garden area.

We arrived on time, and were immediately seated at a table overlooking the garden filled with a variety of gorgeous roses, snapdragons, and petunias. We had a fabulous meal, very fattening desserts and a wonderful time. We paid our bill, and then strolled down the cobblestone streets popping in and out of all the quaint little boutiques, meandering around, looking at the jewelry and clothing and trying not to spend too much money. When we had enough of shopping, we headed over to David Ryan's Pub.

The place was packed as we squeezed our way to the bar where we ordered mudslides, those delicious gooey drinks that go right to your thighs as well as your head. As the bartender served us, I noticed the girl seated next to me was crying. I put my hand on her arm and asked with great concern, "What's wrong?"

"Oh, I'll be alright", she said wiping away her tears. "I just had a big fight with my mother. I'm down here with my family and they're all treating me like shit. All my sister wants me for is to baby sit her kids, I don't have any friends here with me and to top it all off my mother told me she hated me." She looked so upset and so sad.

"How could your mother say such an awful thing to her own daughter? That's terrible! I feel so bad for you. What did your dad say about all this?"

"My Dad's been really nice to me. He just wants us to patch things up, but I can't take it anymore. I just wish my friends were here with me. Last year I had a great time on the Vineyard."

"Well, you can hang out with us for the weekend. Now you instantly have four new friends."

"Gee, that's so nice of you."

"My name is Marianne, and that's Beth, Pam, and Patti."

"Hi, my name is Madeline." And with that I put my arm around her and we all toasted to our new friendship.

Madeline, as it turned out, was a very interesting lady. She was a film scriptwriter from Los Angeles. Being with her was a pleasure. We went to the beach together, had lunch together, hung out at the pool and when evening fell we partied all around town. Saturday we made plans to go to a NRBQ concert in Oaks Bluff, the next town over. NRBQ was one of my favorite bands back in the Seventies. We all decided to go over to The Wharf Pub before the concert. A few minutes after we arrived seven guys from Boston walked in. They immediately started to entertain us, telling us jokes that had us in stitches. Then Ken, the burly one said, "Let's sing a song for the girls."

"Which one should we sing?" his friend shouted out.

"Let's sing God Bless America." And with that they started to sing at the top of their lungs. That became quite contagious because within no time the whole bar was singing God Bless America as loudly as they could! It was phenomenal. The joy, the spirit, and the energy in that room was unbelievable. It was something I shall never forget, only adding to the fabulous time we were already having on the wonderful Island of Martha's Vineyard.

The next day, sadly our last, we decided to make it our best. We rented bikes in the afternoon to explore the island,

and with every turn, discovered something marvelous. We stopped our biking at a huge estate where we spotted two llamas on the grounds. By acting quite silly but having spirited fun, we began whistling, waving, and calling these llamas over to us. Within minutes we actually persuaded these huge, very hairy creatures to come up to the front of the fence. They were a sight to marvel at.

We talked to the llamas for a while and then got back on our bikes and rode down a wooded road where there were scores of rabbits dashing across our path. I never saw so many wild rabbits at one time. I knew they were prolific creatures but this was ridiculous. It made quite a magical day.

We could see the congestion up ahead as we rode our bikes single file into the center of town. With the bikes wedged between the cars and the pedestrians we slowly rode back to Vineyard Bike Rentals, checked in the bikes and started walking back to the hotel. Wiping the sweat from my forehead, I turned to Beth and said, "That was some workout, I'm beat."

"We should take a quick dip in the pool now to revitalize ourselves for our last night on the town," she replied.

"Excellent idea, let's quickly run up to the room and get into our suits."

The water was refreshing, and afterwards we stretched out on the lounge chairs. I began to doze off when I felt a nudge on my shoulder. "Go away," I said, as I placed a towel over my head and rolled over.

"Dinner at the Starbuck's tonight, the most exclusive spot on the island. Wouldn't want to leave you behind," Pam said as she slipped on her sandals and gathered up her magazines and towels.

"The coffee place???"

"No, it just has the same name. This is a five-star French restaurant.

"Okay, I'm coming," I said struggling to rise. "I'll meet you upstairs." I was a little pissed off at Pam, as usual, from a conversation we had earlier in the day at the beach. She told me that things might not work out between Robert and me, so I should try to meet other people. Why does she have to be so negative? I should have told her off then but I didn't. I feel hurt when she says these things, but then I don't react. I shut down. I repress it; thinking just let it go. But it doesn't go away, it builds up and I've been stewing about it all day. Maybe I'll clear the air with her later.

Surprisingly, Pam and I finished dressing first, so we told Patti and Beth we would meet them at the restaurant. We walked into the main dining area, which was very plush with dark mahogany wainscoting, beautifully coordinated drapery and upholstered chairs. We approached the hostess. "We have a reservation for 8:00 p.m. under the name Thompson."

She looked down at the reservation list and said, "Your table isn't quite ready yet, would you like to wait in our lounge area?"

"That would be fine, because the rest of our party has yet to arrive," I said and we began walking toward the lounge. I ordered a glass of wine and Pam had a Bloody Mary. Shortly thereafter, Patti and Beth caught up with us and we were seated at the table. The waiter handed us only two menus, saying he would return soon with the other two.

"Hey girls, isn't this a beautiful dining room?" Patti asked as she opened her menu.

"It really is but it seems a tad stuffy in here, the Locust

Valley Lockjaw crowd seems to have descended on the place," I replied through clenched teeth, for exaggeration. The conversation began to flow and we were all having a blast, laughing and reminiscing about the wonderful vacation we were having. I suppose we were getting a bit loud with all that fun. "We had better calm down; the stiffs two tables away are giving us the eye," I whispered to the girls.

Fifteen minutes went by and we still had not received extra menus, nor water nor bread. "With these prices, you'd think the service would be a little faster," Beth said shaking her head. "I know, this is ridiculous," I said as I raised my hand to get the attention of a passing waiter. All to no avail. "I think we should tell the hostess of our situation," I added.

"I'm with you, I'm hungry. Ask the hostess if she could send the waiter around," Patti replied. I did so and a few minutes later, a very young waiter handed us the additional two menus and took our order for a bottle of Chardonnay. Five minutes later the busboy came to pour water, but he missed a glass, spilling the water all over the tablecloth. Then he brought the rolls and dropped them on the floor. As he fumbled, picking up the rolls off the floor we were trying hard to contain ourselves. A few seconds after he left saying he'd be back with fresh rolls, we all started to laugh.

"This place is a comedy of errors. This is funny," I said smiling.

A minute later the waiter came with the bottle of wine. As he struggled to get the bottle uncorked, he began having a coughing fit, not bothering to cover his mouth. He filled the glasses and left.

"A little influenza with our wine, girls?" Beth said and with that, everybody started having a laughing fit.

"One thing that is definitely infectious around here is

the laughter," Patti said. We were all in stitches; holding our bellies, tears trickling from our eyes. We were getting quite silly. Nothing was that funny; but the laughter was contagious.

We calmed down when the appetizers arrived shortly thereafter and they were delicious. We all wanted a second glass of wine, so we ordered another bottle.

The food was really superb, exquisite cuisine. We all felt things were starting to smooth out. After twenty minutes passed, I asked a busboy why the wine was taking so long. He told me he would speak to the waiter. A minute later the hostess approached the table, "Your main course will be out shortly, but I am sorry to inform you that it is the consensus of the management that you have had too much to drink, so therefore we will not be serving you the additional bottle of wine."

The whole table was shocked, mouths dropping in disbelief.

"Excuse me, but we are not drunk. We just happen to be having a little bit of fun at this table. We have had only one glass of wine each. My cousin and I each had one cocktail in the lounge. None of us had anything to drink before we entered this establishment, and I can't believe we are being treated this way. I would like to speak to the owner of this restaurant," I said seething.

"I'm sorry that won't be possible. He's not here right now. After you finish your main course, we might be able to serve you a second bottle of wine."

"That's ridiculous. Girls, what do you want to do? Do you want to have our main course?"

The mood at the table had taken a major nosedive and everyone wanted to leave.

"Just bring us the check. We won't be having dinner in this restaurant and, I would also like the name of the owner and address where I can write to him." The hostess left saying she would be back with the check.

We all sat back in our chairs dumbfounded. "I don't believe this. It's embarrassing," I said, steam coming out of my ears.

"I guess we were too loud," Beth replied.

"We were having fun. Was that such a crime? I guess the upper crusty crowd couldn't handle it," I added.

"I think the waiters were mad because we complained about them," Patti added.

"That could be it," Pam replied. "And I also don't think this would have happened if we were a table of two couples as opposed to four women."

"You're probably right," I said.

"I only had one glass of wine and I was humiliated for no reason at all," Beth said in total disgust.

"Pam and I only had two drinks. That's nothing considering we both have hollow legs," I said in a puff of laughter. But the situation just wasn't funny anymore. The hostess came back with the check and we took down the name and address of the owner and left in a huff.

We wound up at the Navigator, ordered mudslides and then proceeded to get BOMBED! We asked the hostess for menus but she informed us the kitchen was closed. An empty stomach, aggravation and mudslides are the formula for disaster and that's just what happened after my wonderful cousin began to open her mouth. She turned to me and said, "Now I'm going to tell you something that's going to make you mad."

"Well that's nice Pam, why would you want to tell me

something that you know will make me mad?"

"You know, when we were at the restaurant waiting to be served, you shouldn't have raised your hand to get the waiter's attention."

"Excuse me Pam, but that's how you get a waiter's attention. There is nothing wrong with that. What are you trying to blame this on me now? I am so sick of you and your insults! You are nothing but negative energy! Just get away from me, Pam, just leave!" I said with so much rage I could hardly contain myself.

"No, I'm not going to leave."

"Well fine, if you don't leave, I'll leave," and with that I got up and walked over to the bar and sat down. Madeline had met us at the Navigator and she immediately got up and followed.

"Listen, don't let your cousin get you down like this. There was nothing wrong with raising your hand to get the waiter's attention. Just don't listen to her."

"I can't stand her anymore. She always has a comment, an insult, a dig, and I just can't take it anymore." And as I finished my sentence, who winds up right beside me but Pam. "Get away from me Pam! Just get away!" I said with my neck and face turning beet red.

"Oh come on you're just over reacting. Besides I only tell you these things for your own good."

"PAM, JUST GET AWAY FROM ME!"

Pam wasn't going anywhere. She continued standing right next to me and every time she opened her mouth I became more and more enraged. "Okay Pam, if you won't leave, I will." I then picked myself up and walked out of the restaurant.

Pam got back to the room at about one-thirty. When I

heard her enter the room my anxiety level escalated as I lay in my bed with stomach churning. Then she started in again, this time it was about Robert. "You know, there was a nice crowd at the Wharf. If you came with us you could have met someone new."

"I'm in love with Robert."

"What do you know about love?"

"WHAT DO I KNOW ABOUT LOVE? WHAT DO YOU KNOW ABOUT LOVE, PAM? YOU WERE A BATTERED WIFE!! WHAT'S LOVE PAM? IS LOVE WHEN YOUR HUS-BAND BEATS YOU AND SENDS YOU TO THE HOSPITAL? IS THAT LOVE PAM?"

I was so angry, screaming on top of my lungs that I got up and raised my hand, so enraged I was about to strike her when she twisted my wrist. I backed down, sat on the bed and said, "Pam we can't be friends anymore. I just can't be friends with you anymore." I laid back totally drained, totally saddened at what had just happened. I had never been so enraged in my entire life.

The next morning we woke up and she started in again. "You know, you just over-react to everything."

"Pam, I told you last night, I can't be your friend any-more," I said to her very calmly.

"But why?"

"Pam, this friendship is just not working."

"Why can't you forgive me?" she pleaded. "Winslow said mean things to you, why can you forgive Winslow and not me?"

"Pam, it's just not going to work."

"I'm willing to forget about the whole thing, why can't you just forget about it?"

"I'm sorry Pam. Maybe you're a better person than I am,

being able to get over this so quickly but I just can't. I'm going out to get some breakfast now, I'll see you later." I was so upset as I walked up Main Street to look for a place to have a light breakfast. I found a little deli with a seating area, ordered scrambled eggs on a roll and some juice and sat down feeling totally miserable about what had transpired last night. It was a horrible fight. The worst I had ever had.

Feeling so bad about what had happened, I decided to stop in the small, but very beautiful church I spotted on my way back to the hotel. I walked in, knelt down and said a prayer asking God to forgive me for that horrific fight, and to help me remain calm, and to help me solve my problems. The vacation had been the best of times and the worst of times. Maybe I could learn something from this terrible end to a glorious vacation.

On my way out of the church I noticed a small shelf against the wall that displayed an assortment of small pamphlets. As I browsed through the literature, I spotted one entitled *Adult Children of Alcoholics--Hope, Help, and Healing.* Maybe there's something in here for me, I said as I picked up the pamphlet, put it in my pocketbook and walked back to the hotel.

I got back to the room and began packing when Pam said to me, "I just want to say one thing, I think you are a very kind and generous person and I suppose I'm pretty an-tagonistic. I don't know why I'm like that but I suppose recognizing it is the first step."

"Pam, that's really nice of you to say. Thanks," I said as I put my arms around her and gave her a hug, wondering if our friendship could ever be the same.

We finished packing and it was time to say good-bye to

the island of Martha's Vineyard. Even though there was troble in Paradise it had certainly been mem orable. As we were driving home, I had a nagging anxiety about that fight. Maybe Pam had a point, when she asked me why I could forgive Winslow after he had said cruel things to me and yet not forgive her. I just couldn't figure that one out. The ride home was very long and it dragged.

What a relief it was to finally lie in my own bed. There's nothing like your own bed. I said my prayers and then decided to read the *Adult Children of Alcoholics* pamphlet I had picked up at the church.

I began reading the section entitled *Inside Every Adult is a Child* and I became quite startled when I came to a story about a guy named Tom who went to a party where his friend began to tease him. He became so enraged by his friends teasing that he felt like punching his tormentor, but instead he left the party. He couldn't understand why he wasn't able to just brush off his friend's teasing and his emotional response worried him. Then out of the blue came a memory.

Tom recalled a childhood day when his older brother mercilessly teased him when he cried after his dog was killed by a hit-and-run driver. The memory of the incident washed over Tom like a wave. With it came the insight that his anger at the party was the anger and hurt of the little boy inside of him who needed comfort and understanding so many years ago.

I think I'm being *Zapped* again. This story is a replica of the fight I had with Pam at The Navigator. Only for me it's women who say cruel things to me that make me so upset.

One time I fell apart at work when a female co-worker said something cruel to me. I cried for half a day. My mother said cruel things to me. God she was so mean when she was drunk.

Cruel women remind me of my mother.

Just then a childhood memory came to me. I was about six or seven years old. My father was yelling at my mother saying "How could you say that to your own daughter?" Crying uncontrollably, I ran up the stairs to my room. I was sobbing so hard I could hardly breathe, gasping for air and crying at the same time, almost sounding like I had the whooping cough.

My father came up the stairs, sat down next to me and when he tried to comfort me I asked, "Daddy, why is Mommy so mean?" He turned to me and said, "Your mother is sick. She has a disease, she's an alcoholic and doesn't know what she's saying." I could do nothing but continue to sob uncontrollably.

"Now calm down, try to stop crying," he said, patting my back. "I can't stop, Daddy, I can't stop." I cried and cried and cried.

I don't remember what my mother said to me back then. I have never been able to remember what she said to me.

Then another memory struck me. I was thirty and severely depressed, suicidal. It was right after that big blow-out I had with my boss, Steve. I lost my job, found another, but had absolutely no confidence in myself. With my self-esteem at an all-time low, I couldn't design anymore so I quit this latest job without having another one to go to. Besides that, the man I was dating had just dumped me.

What a mess: totally despondent, totally without hope, seeing only darkness in front of me. My sister with whom I had been living at the time, called my mother and father to take me home for a while. One night I got up to go to the bathroom when a minute later my mother got up too. The door was slightly ajar, and as she began to push it open, I said, "I'm in here." In her drunken voice my mother screamed, "THE HELL WITH YOU!" She was so cruel--- here I was home because I was suicidal, in total despair and she said that to me. How could she have been so mean? She got me so upset, the next day I went into the medicine cabinet, grabbed a handful of my father's Valium, took the train home, and that night I washed down the pills with three or four very strong, double vodka and tonics. Luckily, I was found by my sister and rushed to the hospital just in time, surviving the whole ordeal.

As I lay in my bed now, remembering those very painful moments in my life, I thought, my God, she was cruel. Then my mind raced back to the first childhood memory, then forward to my suicide attempt and back to the memory of me crying as a small child; my thoughts raced back and forth, back and forth. OH MY GOD! OH MY GOD! OH MY GOD! I remember what my mother said to me when I was a little girl. MY MOTHER TOLD ME TO GO TO HELL! SCREAMS OF TERROR ARE POURING OUT OF ME. AAHHHHHHHHHH! SPONTANEOUS, UNCONTROLLABLE SCREAMS, SCREAMS OF TERROR. OH MY GOD, OH MY GOD, The neighbors are going to call the police if I don't stop screaming. I quickly grabbed my pillow and put it over my mouth. There are no tears only these SCREAMS OF TERROR. AHHHHHHHH AHHH, AHHHH, AHHHHHHHH!! AAAAHHHHHHHHHHHHH!!! I can't stop, I can't stop...What's happening to me? Calm down, calm down, calm down, I said to myself still holding the pillow over my mouth. My face is red hot, I'm burning up. Why can't I stop screaming?

An hour passed and finally my screams began turning

into tears. Oh my God, I've never experienced anything so horrifying in my whole life. Complete and utter terror in remembering what my mother said to me when I was a little girl.

As I lay in bed crying, I thought about what a psychologist had once said to me. She told me I had no compassion for myself in what I had endured throughout my childhood. I now found that compassion for myself as I lay in my bed thinking, My God, I was only a baby, six or seven years old and here my mother was telling me to *"Go to Hell."* Unconsciously I carried that right into my adulthood. That's why I am so sensitive to women who say cruel things to me.

When my mother said that again to me twenty-five years later, that is when I took the action and actually attempted suicide instead of just contemplating it. That statement was the emotional trigger that set the action in motion.

And for the past ten years I have been carrying around all this guilt about my suicide attempt. It's been ten long years, and I have never been able to forgive myself for attempting suicide, always wondering how could I ever tell a lover of my past, always feeling so ashamed of what I did and always feeling like damaged goods.

When my tears subsided, I was finally able to forgive myself and realized that my suicide attempt was cause and effect. It was bound to happen sooner or later with all the emotional baggage I'd been carrying around. Ten years later I finally realized that it wasn't my fault. The guilt that had eroded my very being was now gone, replaced with compassion for the hurt little girl inside me. I wondered how different my life would have been if I had had a healthy mother, one who nurtured her child. How different would my relationships be today? How much easier would life be with healthy self-esteem, with confidence in my abilities? When you are raised by an alcoholic parent, you are handicapped. Everything becomes a hundred times harder.

I looked at the clock, 3:30 a.m. I am so tired I thought as I finally rolled over and fell asleep.

The next morning I looked terrible. My eyes were swollen, my throat was sore, voice hoarse, but somehow I managed to get ready for work. Just as I shut the front door behind me my neighbor Deb was leaving her apartment.

"Hi, Marianne. How are you? Did you hear the screams on Greenwich Avenue last night?"

Startled and totally embarrassed, I answered, "No, I didn't hear anything."

Just as I predicted my neighbor heard my screams last night.

"Well, your apartment is more toward the back so I guess you wouldn't have heard them. It sounded awful, like a woman was getting beat up. Anyway, have a good day."

"You too, Deb."

When I got to the office, I told Kathy what had happened the night before.

"Oh, Marianne, I am so sorry," she said and began consoling me with such compassion and empathy; she truly is the kindest person I have ever met. "But you know Marianne, this will probably be good for you. You have to get it all out." She was right. It was good to get it out. My voice was hoarse for a couple of days but after it healed and I settled down, I noticed an extreme reduction of anxiety. My free-floating anxiety had subsided and the days ahead felt like I was walking on air.

God really was helping me to solve my problems. It was

very painful to experience the surfacing of that blocked memory but it was the key that unlocked the reasons for some of my behaviors. Pandora's Box. Well, I did ask God to help me solve my problems. You asked for it and you got it!

   Shortly thereafter I felt compelled to tell my story. I wanted to reach out to other adult children of alcoholics. I picked up the *Greenwich Time* and found an Al-Anon meeting was being held on Wednesday. This is an organization for people who live with alcoholics. I was looking for an Adult Children of Alcoholics meeting but couldn't find one in town. They are closely related and I knew my message would be important to both.

   The last time I went to an Al-Anon meeting I was eighteen-years-old. I was scared and couldn't contain my grief. I entered the room, nervously sat down and when it was my time to speak the tears poured out of me. "My mother's an alcoholic", I said, crying so hard I could barely get the words out. "I'm afraid I'm going to *turn into one*. I go to clubs on the weekends with my friends and drink. They say that the disease is inherited and I'm so petrified that it's going to happen to me. I feel doomed," I said wiping my tears.

   An older man sitting next to me handed me a tissue and then compassionately put his arm around me and said, "Not everyone inherits the disease. You just have to be careful. Watch your drinking and you'll be okay."

   That was twenty-two years ago. To this day I still worry. I worry about everything. "What If," is my middle name. This happens to be a trait of Adult Children of Alcoholics. One of the molds I fit into. My friends were always trying to comfort me, telling me, "You're not going to turn into an alcoholic. Stop worrying so much, there's nothing wrong with partying on the weekends." This weekend's drinking was definitely out of control. I abused alcohol.

Anyhow, I sat down and started to prepare my speech for the Al-Anon meeting on Wednesday. I had to get my message across. I couldn't believe I was brave enough to do this. I hated public speaking. I took a course in it while in college and it was absolutely terrifying to stand in front of class and make a speech. My hands shook like a jackhammer; my voice croaked like a frog, I was a mess.

This time was different. I was nervous but determined. As I entered the room people were mulling around the coffee station, pouring themselves a cup and then taking a seat in the circle of chairs in the middle of the room.

When my turn to speak came I said, "I have something I feel I must share with all of you. I had an experience a few weeks ago that was a significant breakthrough for me. I am hoping that my experience could help someone else."

I then told them of the sheer terror brought on by my remembering the blocked memory and how the words of my mother were the emotional trigger for my suicide attempt twenty-five years later.

"But as painful as it was, that blocked memory was a Godsend. To finally feel compassion and understanding for myself was a miracle. I enveloped the hurt child inside me. I discovered and felt for the first time a genuine self-love, which as the song goes, truly is The Greatest Love of All. So go home and sing yourselves a love song because you all deserve the best that life has to offer."

The woman sitting next to me rubbed my back, knowing that wasn't easy for me to do. "That was very brave of you.

It was wonderful," she said.

People came up to me after class, shook my hand and thanked me for coming and sharing my experience. One guy said, "That really helped me connect with an experience I had with my father. You've helped me understand something about a problem I've had for years."

I was glad to get my message across.

GULLIVER'S TRAVELS

I hadn't heard from Robert since I arrived back from Martha's Vineyard so I broke *The Rules* and called him. He gave me a big hello and told me he was totally swamped lately. "I owe you," he said.

"You really have been working hard."

"Yeah, yesterday I was at the office until ten, went home, worked until two and had to get up at five-thirty. I've been working around the clock. We're gearing up for the testing of the three hundred thousand homes in New York City that we should be starting at the end of August."

"You're going to get sick working that hard. You can't keep that pace up forever."

"I know it will just be for a little while longer. The Griffin Group is in this week and as a matter of fact I was just off to a dinner meeting when you called, but we can talk for a little while."

I then began telling him about my vacation at Martha's

Vineyard, including the story about the llamas on the estate, the guys that sang us God Bless America and my new friend Madeline. We laughed and joked around and then I said "Have you done anything besides work lately?"

"Well, I went to see the movie Forest Gump."

"I can't believe you went to see Forest Gump without me!"

"Well you weren't around, I had a little extra time on my hands so I went to see it. I loved it. I am Forest Gump."

"I really wanted to see that movie with you," I said in a whiney, disappointed voice.

"Well maybe if you stop whining. I could see the movie again."

"Wendy's my name, Whining's my game," I said with a giggle.

"Ah, yes. Wendy Whiner. She was my favorite character from Saturday Night Live."

We continued talking probably for a half hour until Robert said, "I hate to cut you off but I'm already late for my dinner meeting. I'm sorry. I owe you. I'll talk to you soon."

"Good luck with your meeting. Don't forget about me."

I hung up the phone. Five minutes later it rang again. It was my father. "Hi Dad, How you doing?"

"PUT ON JEOPARDY!" he said in his usual loud voice. My father is a little hard of hearing and also a real character.

"What do you mean put on Jeopardy? Is that why you called me up?"

"I don't know. Just put on Jeopardy."

I put the T.V. on and a second later, Alex Tribec asked the Final Double Jeopardy question under the category Famous Writers.

"What is the answer to this question posed by an 18th Century writer? And who was the writer? A man has three faces. He looks in the mirror and what does he see? Players we'll give you a few minutes to write your answer while we go to a commercial."

"That's really a strange question Daddy. What made you call me up and tell me to put on Jeopardy?"

He let out a chuckle and said, "I don't know I just was sitting here watching the show and felt like calling you."

"But you rarely call me. You don't like to pay for the long distance"

A minute later Alex Tribec came back on. "Okay panelists, the question was...A man has three faces. He looks in the mirror and what does he see? The answer is Nothing. And that was written by Jonathan Swift.

"What does that mean Daddy?"

"I don't know what that means."

"That really intrigues me. What did Jonathan Swift write, Daddy?"

"I don't know." Then changing the subject he asked, "So, what else is new?"

I began telling him about my adventures on Martha's Vineyard and the latest news in my life. My father is such a nice guy and funny, too. Thank God I had my father when I was growing up.

When I climbed into bed that evening, I thought about JEOPARDY and said to myself I have to find out what book Jonathan Swift wrote. I want to find out what that passage means. A man has three faces. He looks in the mirror and what does he see? Nothing. I just can't figure that one out.

A few days later I decided to go to Southport for the day. Southport is another one of those twilight zone towns. Nothing ever changes. The town looks the same now as it did thirty or more years ago.

My love of Connecticut actually comes from my grandmothe who lived in Southport. I have wonderful, warm, sweet, childhood memories from the summers I stayed at her home. My sisters and I would spend two weeks every summer at Grammy's. Poppy's and Grammy's. Nothing better than that.

There was Jimmy's Candy Store, The Spic and Span Market and the Old Barber Shop all in the center of town. It's the quintessential New England town with white clapboard buildings with black shutters and cobblestone sidewalks. White picket fences and hundred-year-old oak trees. A nickel bought you five pieces of penny candy from Jimmy's and a dollar would buy you a hot dog and fries at Rawley's Hot Dog Stand. Rawley's was as famous for its hot dogs as it was for all the initials carved into the old beat-up wooden tables they had inside. Every young lover, hopeful lover or rambunctious kid just had to carve their initials into the table after they chowed down a dog and fries.

They were wonderful times.

It was great to be back in town. I attended services at the local Episcopalian Church, and decided it would be nice to have lunch at the harbor so I stopped at Jimmy's Deli to pick up a sandwich. On the ride over to the harbor I passed by the Pequot Library where they were having a Book Sale. Maybe I could find a book written by Jonathan Swift, I thought as I parked the car.

There were tents on the front lawn of the library with row after row of tables of old books for sale. Entering one of the tents I asked the woman cashier, "What type of books did Jonathan Swift write?"

"Classics. That would be over in the Main Building," She said pointing in the direction of the beautiful stone building to the left. I walked over making my way through the crowds to enter the library and asked to be directed to the room where the classics were. Books were set up on tables, so I began rifling through looking for Jonathan Swift. I couldn't find any books by him at first but others caught my interest and I started picking out an assortment of well-known classics such as *Catcher in the Rye* and found books written by just about every author except Jonathan Swift.

I kept searching and rifling through book after book and after about twenty minutes I began to feel a little light-headed. It was hot and dusty in this room, books laid out on these tables in no order whatsoever and I felt sick. I had collected five books, put them down on the cashier's table and asked the man collecting the money, "What book did Jonathan Swift write?"

"*Gulliver's Travels*," He replied.

"*Gulliver's Travels!*" I said with welcome surprise. Would you have a copy of that?"

"We should have a copy on that table right over there," he said pointing to the table I had just come from.

"Oh," I said with my spirits spiraling downward. "Well, can I leave these books here while I go back to look?"

"Sure."

I put the books down to walk toward the table thinking I'm going to get sick if I have to look through those books again. A second later, a woman eight feet away said to me in a raised voice, "Excuse me Miss, my daughter has a copy of *Gulliver's Travels* in her hand. She'll give it to you right now if you'd like."

Totally surprised the cashier said, "Wow! That's really

nice of you! But are you sure your daughter doesn't want it?"

"No, that's alright. She can give her the copy," the woman replied.

Startled, I looked at the little girl who was standing right in front of me and felt a twinge of guilt since her expression didn't indicate she wanted to give up that book too quickly. She sadly looked down, and handed it to me. "Are you sure you don't want it?" I asked.

"No, it's okay," she said finally with the glimmer of a smile.

"Gee, thanks!" I said with a smile as wide as it could get, so relieved that I wouldn't have to go over to that table again.

"That was really nice! You're a lucky young lady," The cashier said as I handed him a grand total of two dollars and fifty cents for all six books.

What a strange experience. That was bizarre. Jonathan Swift was coming at me in very peculiar ways. First my father called me up out of the clear blue telling me to put on Jeopardy and then this woman's daughter handed me the book just as I was about to give up looking.

Weird. Very weird.

I think I was just *Zapped* again with one of those strange coincidences. I wondered if there was a message in that book for me.

The next day, I pulled up a chair in Kathy's office, leaned back and said, "You know he hasn't called me lately, Kathy. I called him last week and he was really nice, told me he was swamped and that he owes me, but I'm getting a little depressed about this whole thing."

"Marianne, this deal he's putting together is really big. My husband works on Wall Street and he heard about the deal. Right now this is his life. I'm sure he'll call you soon. You have to give him time. My God, he's been working on this for ten years and it's all finally coming together for him. Just be patient, he'll come around."

"I hope so. I'm really crazy about him, Kathy."

"Don't worry sweetie, he'll call.

I went home that evening feeling better after having had my little talk with Kathy and decided that maybe I should send a little care package to Robert at the office.

I started my Care Package by gathering up a few pictures from Martha's Vineyard; there was one of the girls together. I took out some blank white narrow stick-on labels, attached one to the bottom of that photo and entitled it "The Women of Martha's Vineyard." I then picked out a picture of me with the llamas. I didn't look very good in the photo; my hair was all screwed up, so I labeled that photo "Marianne having a bad hair day with Dali Llama." The third picture was a view of the harbor from our balcony. I labeled that one "A Day in Paradise."

I went to the stationery store, bought a blank card with an angel on it and a small bag of Hershey's Kisses. Then I went to the Health Food Store and bought an energizing Power Bar and a bottle of liquid B-12. I had been using that stuff when I got tired at the office and it really gave me a boost of energy. That night I started to put together my little Care Package. I wrote inside the card "May All Your Dreams Come True." Then I began to write Robert a Love Letter...

July 24, 1994

Dear Robert, (aka King of the Dragon Slayers)

Hope this little care package helps to energize and cheer you up during your stay on Planet Omega. Looking forward to your visit to Planet Venus where I would like to Hug You, Kiss you, Touch you, and Ravage you!

I miss you and would love to see you but, it seems at this time it is too difficult for you to concentrate on the business and see me as well. Therefore, I am now learning how to handle this with grace. I hope you like this little surprise because, doing fun things for you makes me happy. So, don't worry about me, do what you have to and when you're ready, I'll meet you on Planet Venus.

Love,
Marianne XXXOOO

I got a small box and lined it with tissue paper. Enclosed in the Care Package was the letter, the Hershey's Kisses, the Power Bar, and the Liquid B-12. I then sprinkled everything with a confetti of Silver Stars. I then carefully added a top layer of tissue paper, put the top on the box, wrapped it with brown paper and meticulously addressed it to Robert's office. I really had a lot of fun putting this package together. I hoped he'd get a kick out of it. The next morning as I walked down the Avenue to the train station, I stopped off at the Post Office to mail it, hoping to hear from Robert soon.

That evening which was Friday, Beth, Patti and I were going out on the town. I didn't want to go to Brett's. I was so sick of that place. I made a call to the girls and told them so. We decided to start out in Southport at the Sonoma Grill the new hot spot in the area. It's touted as a California Grill where the food is prepared in an open view. They also have a large bar area where you can order light fare during happy hour, which is exactly what we did. We had a bite to eat, a couple of drinks and we were off to the second spot, The Horseshoe Tavern in Southport. I wanted to go there because I remembered having lunch there as a small child when we went to visit my grandmother. The place was exactly the same, except for the reupholstering of the booths.

We stayed for half an hour had one drink and were off to the next place, The Boxing Cat in Old Greenwich, the place where I met Robert.

Oh my God, I feel like I might see him tonight.

We walked into the Boxing Cat but I was wrong, he wasn't there.

"Well girls, what do you think?" Patti asked.

"Looks like a geriatric crowd tonight," Beth replied.

"I guess you don't want to stay," I said.

"Nah, let's go someplace else." Patti replied.

"Well, where do you want to go?" I asked.

"Let's go to Brett's. There's live music there."

"Brett's, I hate Brett's. I don't want to go to Brett's."

"Oh come on, there's no place else to go around here."

"Well, I guess so. I can't believe we are going to Brett's."

When we got back into the car driving down Route 1,

the feeling that I was going to see Robert came back to me. No, he's probably working I thought. As we walked into the place the feeling got stronger. I knew he was going to be there. But, when I looked around, I didn't see him.

"I'm going to the ladies room girls," I said as I walked up the stairs. I touched up my make-up before heading back and when I was halfway down *there was Robert.*

I walked over, gave him a big smile and said "Hi Honey! How are you?"

"I should put my head down in shame. I wasn't sup-posed to see you tonight. I just left the office. The group that's playing tonight sent me a CD and they want to be on Omega Sound. I only came in to have a drink and listen to their music."

"That's okay, I understand," I said as I put my arms around Robert and gave him a gentle kiss. "Are you alone?" I asked.

"Of course I'm alone. What do you think, I have a little man in my pocket?" Robert said as he took his hand parting the breast pocket of his suit and peering inside of it.

I let out a giggle. That's so funny, I thought, maybe he's Gulliver. Weird, very weird.

"Can I buy you a drink?" he asked.

"Sure, I'll have a white wine," I said and Robert turned around to order the drinks. A minute later he handed me my wine.

"So what are you doing here? Just out with the girls?"

"Yeah, and look, I have on the same outfit I was wearing when I met you," I said looking down at my Chambray denim shirt with a white tank top underneath, jeans and khaki colored cloth sneakers.

"I know. You're dressed to kill again."

I giggled again, thinking he's so cute when I realized I hadn't introduced Robert to the girls. They were standing to the side of us and were probably wondering who I was talking to. "Let me introduce you to my friends," I said as I gently tugged his arm.

"Girls, this is The Omega Man."

"You're the Omega Man?" Patti asked with eyes wide open and jaw dropped.

Robert smiled. "What have you been telling your friends about me?"

"Just how wonderful you are. You're The Omega Man," I replied, looking up at Robert with loving eyes and a smile.

He chuckled and asked, "Is there a telephone booth around here?"

We laughed then moseyed over to the bar. I spotted an open chair-- I have radar for these things. No matter how crowded it is, I always get a seat. We talked for a while, nuzzling each other until I finally asked, "How's Merv? Is he still around?"

"Yeah, they're still around and to tell you the truth, I'm getting sick and tired of it, so I'm taking off to Lake Placid for a few days."

My jaw dropped. I was in utter shock. He's going to Lake Placid and he hasn't seen me for three weeks.

"What's the matter?" Robert asked.

"Nothing." I replied, thinking maybe he just needs time to be alone. The business sounds like it's really getting to him. I'm not going to mention anything. We continued fooling around and nuzzling. A half hour went by when I had to go to the ladies room.

When I returned Robert, still standing by my chair, was talking to another girl. I sat down, and lit up a cigarette as

Robert continued talking to this girl. Steam was coming out of my ears. Then out of the corner of my eye, I saw the girl move around the other side to order a drink and I turned to Robert and said, "I haven't seen you in three weeks and now you're talking to another girl!"

"Marianne," Robert said as if to chastise me while he eyed the woman. Maybe she's with the band, I thought.

"I don't care about her. I'm sorry, but I have to go home. Could you please walk me to my car." I said. He didn't budge.

"Could you please walk me to my car?"

"Okay, I'll walk you to your car."

As we walked, I began cuddling up to Robert, God I was still crazy about him. "I miss you. Let's smooch in the car."

"No really, I can't."

"Come on."

"No really, I can't."

"GET IN THE CAR!" I said nudging him with a smile.

"You are too funny," Robert said as he got in the car. I started nuzzling and he gave me a peck on the lips. I wanted more than just a peck and was getting very depressed at the way Robert was acting. I wasn't getting very good vibes.

I guess it's over I thought as I stared out of the car window and said, "I just sent you a surprise, and I think I'm going to feel like a real jerk."

"What's the surprise?" Robert asked.

"I can't tell you."

"Why are you going to feel like a jerk?" Robert asked.

"Because I don't think you want to go out with me anymore."

Robert looked totally surprised, took his hands, cupped

my face with them and said vehemently, "Marianne!! That's not true!! Don't you know it's only like this because of the type of work I'm doing?"

"But I haven't seen you in three weeks and you don't even want to kiss me."

"The Smoocher doesn't have the energy to kiss the Smoochette. I was up at five, worked until ten and just came down here for a couple of drinks because this band sent me their CD. That woman in the bar is with the band."

"How much longer is it going to take to close the deal for Omega Sound?"

"About ten more days," he said with a sigh.

"Alright." I gave Robert a soft kiss on the lips.

"Now I'm going to go back inside, listen to the band for a few minutes longer, and then I'm going home to bed. I'll talk to you soon. Okay?" he asked again, cupping my face in his hands.

"Okay."

I was sitting at my work table when the receptionist came over the intercom and said, "Marianne, pick up line 6."

"Marianne?"

"Robert, how are you?" I asked knowing he must have gotten my surprise package.

"I'm sitting here with silver stars all over my pants."

"Ahh! You got your surprise! Do you like it?"

"I LOVE IT!"

"I'm so happy you liked it. Did you like the pictures?" I asked.

"They're great. You're so cute."

"Did you try the Liquid B-12? It should really give you a little boost while you're working so hard."

"Yeah, it's pretty good stuff."

"So, I guess you're still pretty busy."

"Yeah, but soon it will all be worth it."

"And what about my letter, did you like that?"

Robert then went into his medieval Knight in Shining Armor accent and said, "Of course, my Love! PROTECT THE PLANET VENUS WHILE I'M GONE! KEEP YOUR LEGS CLOSED!"

With that one I went into hysterical laughter. "You are so funny."

"Well, my Love, I've got to go into a meeting now. Thanks for the great package. I'll talk to you soon."

HOUDINI

I was sitting in front of the boob tube, clicker in hand flipping through the channels and wondering why I hadn't heard from Robert. I figured this could be another disappearing act; a scene that was all too common in the drama of my dating life. I couldn't believe he just didn't care. When he cupped my face in his hands and told me it was only the type of work he is doing that was keeping us apart, I believed him. He seemed genuinely excited when he received my care package, yet it was hard to believe that only the business held him back from seeing me. Why does this always happen to me? I thought this time would be different. Maybe he's scared.

As I slowly rose from my big overstuffed chair, I wondered what was in the fridge for dinner tonight. Robotically, I wandered into the kitchen, opened the freezer compartment to check out my lean selection of Lean Cuisines, when the phone rang. "Hello?"

"Hi, Marianne, it's me Patti, I'm over at Brett's and you better get your ass over here because The Omega Man just walked in."

"I can't believe he's there!"

"Hurry up, get dressed and get over here as fast as you can. I had to sneak by him to the phone booth so when you get here just pretend you were supposed to meet me here. I'm sitting at the far end of the bar."

"Oh God, I can't believe this. Okay, I'll be over in about fifteen minutes."

Shifting to high gear, I freshened up, ironed a shirt in record time and headed out. What was he doing there? He doesn't have time to see me, but he has time for Brett's, I thought. Nervously opening the door to the restaurant, I spotted Robert standing at the front of the bar. As I wandered closer, I pretended to be looking for someone and gave a look of surprise when I saw him. "Well, look who it is. What a *coincidence*. What are you doing here, Robert?"

"I knew you'd be here," he answered, looking a bit nervous.

"I'm supposed to meet my friend Patti here. There she is at the end of the bar," I said with eyes wandering towards Patti. "You remember Patti, why don't you come over and say hello with me?"

"I was just on my way out. Tell your friend I said hello," Robert replied as my heart sank. I bypassed his cold reply and asked in a harsh tone, "Why are you acting this way? Just come over to say hello to her with me."

"Well alright." Robert followed me. I gave Patti a warm hello, reintroduced her to Robert and, the three of us chatted for a few minutes. "Do you want to sit down and have a drink?" I asked Robert. He agreed. I told Patti I'd be back later and Robert and I sat down at a table up front. After a glass of wine and a few minutes of catch up, I decided not to get on his case about his leave of absence. I wanted to see where the evening would naturally lead. Within a short period of time he seemed to be warming up when he asked if I wanted to get a little bite to eat while we were having our cocktails. I agreed, but a few seconds later, Patti stopped by the table and Robert suggested we skip the bar food and invited both of us to dinner in the main dining room. "Wow, that's so nice of you, honey." I said.

We were seated in the garden room with lush plants hanging along the top of the windows. Patti excused herself to go to the ladies room and, as soon as she was out of sight, Robert and I began to cuddle. We held hands, and as we looked into each other's eyes, a long vine of leaves landed on top of my head. Robert laughed. As the waitress came by with menus Robert pointed to my head and said, "She's being attacked by your killer philodendron. Do you think you could clip the culprit?" We all laughed as the waitress obliged and we resumed our cuddling.

"Let's do E.T.," I said to Robert. E.T. was a little game we played the last time I saw him. When we felt funny about kissing in public, Robert would twirl his out stretched index finger and touch the tip of my nose just like E.T. did in the movie.

"Yeah, let's play E.T., that was fun," Robert replied as his finger landed on my nose." I giggled, smiled and said, "E.T. phone home."

"Come closer," Robert said as he pulled my chair closer to him.

"Why?" I asked.

"Because, I love you," Robert said. I looked at him with

body and soul wanting him so badly. "Oh, Robert," I said kissing him lightly on the lips. Patti started walking toward us at that moment and we both straightened up to greet her. The waitress then came by and took our orders as the festivities continued.

I pulled out some photographs of Woodstock II. As we were looking through them Robert said, "You know those pictures you sent me of Martha's Vineyard? They are on my desk."

"Wow! You have my pictures on you desk, honey?"

"Yeah."

"That's so sweet."

The food arrived not a second too soon since we were all famished. Everything was delicious, but I noticed Robert starting to get fidgety as I got up to go to the ladies room. When I returned, the table had been cleared, Patti had gone up front to talk to a friend, the check was on the table and Robert was nervously looking for the waitress. He was in such a hurry to leave that he got up and went to the bar to pay the check.

"What's wrong?" I asked.

"I've got to get going. You know, you and Patti are dangerous women."

"What are you talking about?"

"Nothing, it's just late and I've got to get up early tomorrow." He left a tip on the table, got up and whispered in my ear, "I'll talk to you soon."

I sat there seething as I watched him leave the dining room. This is bullshit, I thought to myself. I'm going to find out what's going on. I got up and walked in the direction of the front door. When I got behind Robert I noticed he was joking with some girls on the way out.

"That's nice," I said steam once again coming out of my ears. Robert turned around and shot me a look of annoyance.

"So now you're giving me dirty looks," I said as we started to walk out the door.

"I'm not giving you dirty looks."

"Listen, I want to know what's going on. For six weeks we went out and everything was wonderful."

"Yes, everything *was* wonderful!" He emphatically replied.

"Then for the next six weeks you don't want to see me, you don't want to talk to me and I want to know what's going on!" I screamed, emotions running wild at this point.

"We saw each other tonight," he replied weakly.

"That was by accident! If it's something besides the business I want to know!"

"It's just the business! It's just the business!"

As we reached his car, my ranting and raving continued. "Listen, all my friends think I'm a jerk waiting around for you! They think I should be dating other people. Now I want to know how you feel!"

He got in his car, shut the door, and said, "Okay, I'll let you know how I feel." He then turned on the radio and a song came on and he began to sing to me. "What ever you want, I'll give it to you... You were the first, you'll be the last"...At this point I calmed down and was enjoying his serenade, bopping to the music and when he finished he said, "There, that's how I feel about you."

"That was nice." I said but I wasn't going to let him get away with this so, I asked. "When am I going to see you again?"

With a terribly pained look on his face, he cried out, "I

don't knowwwwwwwwwwwww!!! I'll call you tomorrow, I'll call you tomorrow," he nervously replied as he started the car and began to pull out of his space.

"Noooooooooooooooooooooo, Don't go, Don't go!" I pleaded, holding on to the car door handle, tears streaming down my cheeks.

"I'll call you tomorrow, I'll call you tomorrow," he said pulling out of the parking lot. I walked home feeling awful.

I just don't understand him. He tells me he loves me but then he bolts from the restaurant. I wish I could believe it was only the business but I know it's not. He must be scared; one of those fear of commitment types. I always wind up with men like that, and now I feel I probably scared him away ranting and raving in the parking lot. Oh God, I've really made a fool of myself. I went to bed feeling totally miserable.

The next day I felt just as bad. I couldn't stop thinking about him. I was totally *OBSESSED!* I dragged myself off to work and spent the whole morning moping around. I went to the bookstore on my lunch hour and did what most Red-Blooded American women do when their relationships are in turmoil...headed for the self-help books. He must have a fear of commitment and I wanted to find out more about it.

Sheepishly, I headed for the psychology section of the store, looking around, hoping no one I knew would be there. This section always gives me a creepy feeling. There's a certain paranoia that comes with perusing self-help books, so I just wanted to get a book and checkout as fast as possible without the cashier eyeing my book and then me. I browsed and came upon one entitled *Men Who Can't Love... How to recognize a commitment-phobic man before he breaks your heart.* Hmm. This is the one. I paid with my head held up high this time; after all this was a book about men.

I got home that night and eagerly began reading. *These men often give mixed signals... "Now you see him, now you don't Houdini. He will disappear and reappear over an extended period of time...*Yep, that's Robert. Then it listed the many ramifications of commitment-phobia... *Making major purchases is often traumatic, although the moment of purchase can be exhilarating, the reality of the decision may bring on anxiety, doubt, and self-flagellation.*

Hey wait a minute that sounds like me! I recently redecorated my apartment and when each piece of furniture I purchased arrived, I wanted to return it. My couch came; I didn't like the color; I called the store and asked if I could exchange it. My rug, I freaked out when I got it home, I wanted to return it. I even wanted to exchange my car for a different color. The anxiety of making these purchases was unbelievable and I continuously put myself down for making so-called wrong decisions. This is a real quirk of mine. People always make light of the fact that I like to buy and return things all the time. The credit department at Bloomingdale's once called me in to discuss the excessive amount of returns on my account. They threatened to close my account.

I think major purchases are also a problem for Robert. He has a 1985 Ford Taurus that he said he was going to run into the ground before he will buy a new car. Now that's pretty weird for a man who's about to be a zillionare.

The book went on to say some of these men like to write in pencil because pen is too permanent. Whenever I wrote up my patterns I used pencil until I got to one company where the head patternmaker came over and told me to write them up in magic marker. He then took a big, black, magic marker and wrote on my pattern with it, which really bothered me. Then the book asked, *Do you own any pets? Typically, the commitment-phobic does not have any pets because owning a pet is a huge commitment.* I never had nor wanted any pets. Robert doesn't have any pets either. *Do you own or rent? The person fearing commitment almost always rents.* I rent and keep putting off buying anything even though my accountant tells me I should. Robert also rents at the age of forty.

Then the book spoke of the commitment phobic job pattern and said it must meet at least one of the following criteria. *It must come under the heading of non-structured where a good example of this would be a self-employed person.* That's Robert. Or the job pattern would come under the heading of non-permanent where these men may never be able to settle into one job and may constantly be moving from job to job. That sounds like me! But, the garment center is a very transient lifestyle, and many people have the same revolving door experience as I have. But, when I was younger, I kept changing colleges; going to four different institutions so this behavior existed before the garment center.

As I read on I was continually surprised at the similarities that existed in myself. *In the beginning, when you first meet, the commitment phobic typically goes into high gear. It's all-hyper, a no-holds-barred come-on. He appears to be totally romantic. But you on the other hand, when you first meet, you don't move so quickly.* Yes I do! I moaned. *You have to be somewhat convinced that his feelings and intentions are sincere before you respond in kind.* No I don't! Oh My God, I think Robert is my male clone! I must have a subliminal fear of commitment. It makes perfect sense. I have to go to a shrink. This is unbelievable.

I turned the page and the following section was entitled, Can Women Be Commitment phobic? Well, this is right up my alley. I read on. *Once you understand the origins of commitment phobia, it would seem only logical that this should not be a gender specific problem. After all, women must be as sensitive to commitment as men, equally fright-ened by the prospect of entrapment?*

The answer to this is both yes and no. Yes, many women are scared of--even terrified by---commitment. Yet, the most powerful force driving a woman to commit has to be her ma-ternal instincts--her biological need to couple and reproduce. The survival of the species depends entirely on the continua-tion of the species, a task that Mother Nature has relegated primarily to women. With a few exceptions, all other fears and desires pale in the face of this most potent biological force.

I finished the book in no time devouring its contents like a piranha devours its prey. When I got to the last page I was numb with the realization that I myself could have a fear of commitment. I then glanced at the back page, which was an advertisement for Important Books for Today's Woman; there was a list of five, the last one being *Slay Your Own Dragons: How Women Can Overcome Self-Sabotage in Love and Work* by Nancy Good. My nickname for Robert was my Dragon Slayer. I always called him that and when I sent him that care package, the salutation read: Dear Robert aka King of the Dragon Slayers.

This is creepy! What is with all these weird coinci-dences? I can't take it anymore. And Robert, I can't believe we have the same problem. We can solve our problems together; I know we can but right now it doesn't even seem like we'll ever see each other again after the way I behaved last night. I have to get on good terms with him. I should write him another letter. I need him to come back. Maybe I should write him another letter. I got out my stationery and began to write....

August 15, 1994

Dear Robert,

Hope all is going well with you. I'm sorry I behaved so badly on Thursday night. Just a bad case of P.M.S. No, I don't think so. I've got it, my wine must have been spiked with Love Potion #9 because, this love business makes people get a little nutty sometimes. Yes, that's true, but they haven't really marketed that stuff yet.

The truth of the matter is that when that clingy, demad ing, whiny, childlike side of me comes out, it's because I'm scared. I get scared that you won't come back or that you really don't care. Let's face it; I didn't get to be 40 and single without having been really hurt before.

Most times I'm pretty good in accepting the fact that you are too busy to see me because of the business. It's hard for me, but in some ways, this time we have had to spend apart has been good for me because I've been recognizing some of my problems lately. I've discovered I have many fears, some of them being a fear of intimacy, and a fear of revealing myself to you. What I'm really trying to say is that sometimes this love business makes me behave poorly, but I hope you still love me because, I still love you.

Love,
Marianne

God, I was so upset. I hoped he would call me when he got the letter. I addressed the envelope and put a stamp on it and looked at the time. It was midnight. I put the letter in my pocketbook so I wouldn't forget it and went to sleep.

I mailed the letter on my morning walk to the station and, during this time, I also decided I had to call my old shrink. If I had a fear of commitment, I wanted to do something about it. The book was right, I didn't have much time left. My biological clock was ticking--very loudly--the sound, as a matter of fact, was deafening.

I arrived at the office, and immediately called the doctor to set up an appointment but she was fully booked and couldn't squeeze me into her schedule. I asked her if she could recommend someone. She asked me if I wanted to see a female or a male therapist and I decided male, since I had so many problems with the male species. She recommended Dr. Jay Harill, said he was a great psychologist and wished me lots of luck. I called. The only appointment he had was a week and a half away. I booked it.

I spent the rest of the morning discussing the book, *Men Who Can't Love*, with my fellow patternmaker, Ida. I told her there was also a section in the book that said these men have peculiar phone behavior sometimes only giving out one number. Robert only gave me his office number. Once I tried calling him at home but, there was no answer and he told me he could usually be reached at the office because that's where he usually is. The book also said some of these men don't have answering machines. I decided to try Robert's home number once again so I picked up the phone and to my surprise this time he had his machine on. I listened and stood frozen in my tracks as I heard, "Hi, you have reached 325-6602. We're not home right now to take your call. Please leave a message at the beep." *We're* not home! Robert told me he lived alone.

"Ida, I don't believe this, Robert's message says, '*We're* not home.' What does that mean?" I asked with a frantic look on my face."

She hesitated and then said, "Maybe it's just phrased that way for business purposes or maybe he's married."

"No, he's not married! He's not married! Maybe he's living with somebody though," I replied feeling weak.

"Give me his home phone number and when I get home tonight, I'll call and ask for Mrs. Brenner. I'll make up some excuse for calling. Let's see, I know, I'll tell him I work for the new Health Club that's opening soon in Stamford for ladies only and I'm offering a free week to try out the club."

"Yeah, that's a good one," I said while writing his phone number on a piece of paper and then handing it to her, hoping my worst fears weren't true.

Later that evening, I called Ida and she said she tried the number but no one was home. I was a nervous wreck. I couldn't stand the waiting. I again called her at about ten o'clock and this time she said she got through. "Bingo, he's married," she said and I was crushed.

"What do you mean he's married? Was she there? Did she tell you she was Mrs. Brenner?" I asked in a panic stricken voice with my heart pounding.

"No, she wasn't home. I called and he answered. I then asked for Mrs. Brenner. His reply was "Who's calling?" I then gave him the Health Club routine and he told me to call back at about eight-thirty."

"Well that still doesn't mean he's married. I say he's living with her."

"What's the difference?" Ida asked with a sigh.

I couldn't believe what I was hearing. I know he's not married. He doesn't love that girl.

I was in shock for the rest of the day. When I arrived home that evening, I poured myself a glass of wine, sat down on my living room chair and thought to myself, how could I be so stupid? All along in the back of my mind I knew it. I knew he was living with someone. I couldn't face it. And to think I just sent him that letter apologizing for my behavior. This whole thing is making me sick. How could he say all those wonderful things to me? He has to break up with her. He doesn't love her. He just needs time to get out of his situation. I know he's not married, he can't be. He'll probably show up at Brett's on Thursday night. That's where he was last Thursday when he told me he loved me and had my pictures on his desk. That's the busiest night there, he knows I'll be there and I bet you a hundred bucks he shows up and that's when I'm going to find out the truth.

It was Thursday night and I was angry. It was showdown night at Brett's. Patti and I entered the saloon and sure enough Two-Timing Robert was sitting at the bar having a bite to eat. I sat on Robert's right, Patti to his left.

"Well look who's here. Hi, Robert, how are you?" I said trying to act casually.

"Hi! How's it going? I'd kiss you hello but I have my mouth full," he said as he continued to eat his salad.

We sat for a while making small talk with him discussing the goings on with Omega Sound. I asked him if he had received my letter and he said, "No, the mail's been awfully slow lately."

He's so full of shit. I know he got that letter. I mailed it a week ago. Half an hour went by and then Robert said, " I have to get going. I have a ton of work to do."

I'm so tired of his bullshit.

"So how's the wife and kids, Robert?" I asked sitting back with arms crossed.

"What are you talking about?" Robert asked in surprise. "I don't have a wife and kids!"

I looked him right in the eye, and asked sternly, "Are you married?"

"No, I'm not!" he answered emphatically.

"Are you living with someone?" I asked, peering directly into his eyes.

"Sometimes. I have a maid."

"I asked you a question. Are you living with someone?"

"I refuse to be interrogated. Every time I come in here you interrogate me."

"Well, then why do you come in here if you know I'll be here?" I asked as Robert looked up at me with these big sad eyes. "Now, I'm asking you again. Are you living with someone?"

"That's none of your business," Robert replied with a

smug attitude.

I was seething and I couldn't believe what I was hearing. "Excuse me, but yes, it is my business! Last week in that room," I said pointing to the dining room, "you told me you loved me and that you had my pictures on your desk. And, yes I do have a right to know if you are living with someone and if I have a future with you."

"Everything you need to know, you will know next week. I am not answering any questions tonight. Now I have to get going. I have a very busy day tomorrow."

What a smug little bastard. "Why should I wait a week? I've waited too long already," I replied in a voice filled with disgust.

"I'm not going to discuss it here. I'll talk to you next week."

"You are unbelievable," I said shaking my head as I watched Robert pay his check. When he walked out of the restaurant, I turned to Patti and said, "He is a lying piece of shit! He's living with someone. You can tell by the way he answered my questions. I have a maid. Do you believe that? The oldest trick in the book. And it's none of my business. He is really fucked up."

I was angry, in shock with my stomach in knots as a result of my latest discovery. I sat there motionless, staring out into space, I knew I should let him go but I couldn't. I then turned to Patti and said with a glimmer of hope, "I wonder why I have to wait a week for him to tell me. Maybe he's going to break up with her."

ON THE COUCH

I drove over the great span of the Throgs Neck Bridge heading home to visit my Dad. The hot sun reflected off the car. When the traffic began to swell, I became very sad thinking about Robert wondering what he would have to say to me next week.

I pulled into the driveway to my dad's house and saw him stretched out on a lounge chair, the newspaper on his lap, taking a nice little snooze in the hot sun. My dad's a sweet guy. As the car door closed, I heard a little stirring coming from the lounge chair. "Hi, Dad. Are you awake?"

"Hmm, yeah, yeah, I'm awake." I went over and gave him a kiss hello and sat down in the chair next to him. We caught up on the news around town, relaxed and just soaked up some sun. I then asked him a question I suspected he might have a negative reaction to.

"Dad, I'd like to go to the Lutheran Church in town this Sunday. I just feel like checking it out. Do you want to go with me?"

"No! I'm a Catholic and I'm going to St. Bernard's. You were raised Catholic and you should go to church with me!"

"Dad, I don't want to go to St. Bernard's. I want to go to the Lutheran Church and that's where I'm going!"

"You do what you want, but I don't think you should go there," he said with a grouchy look and went back to reading his newspaper. "Hey, there's a street fair in Westbury today, why don't we take a ride over there?" he asked, changing the subject.

"Okay, let's go." We got in his car and on the ride there, I began to tell my father about Robert and all the weird coincidences that were happening to me. The strange sermon I heard at Second Congregational Church, the newspaper article, "*The Late Blooming Groom*," discovering I had a fear of commitment through a book I bought to find out about Robert's fear of commitment, and the suggested reading *Slay Your Own Dragons*. I also reminded him of the time he called me and told me to put on Jeopardy with the question about the writing of Jonathan Swift--A man has three faces, he looks in the mirror and what does he see? I told him of the strange way *Gulliver's Travels* landed in my hand at the Pequot Library sale and Robert's bizarre response when I asked him if he was alone, he replied "Do you think I have a little man in my pocket?", having never told him about the *Gulliver's Travels* story. "Dad, these coincidences are scaring me. What do you think they are?"

"I don't know, it's like someone is following you around."

The street fair was a nice way to kill the afternoon. On the way home we picked up some food for dinner. I cooked him a healthy, delicious meal something he rarely does for himself since my mom died. The rest of the evening we spent just lounging around the house and watching a video, when I finally dozed off at about midnight.

I woke up early, and I was glad I did because I wanted to make the nine o'clock service at Good Shepherd Lutheran Church, even without Dad's approval. Why is it that even at the age of forty parents can still make you feel guilty?

I dressed, had a quick bite to eat, and headed out the door, not wanting to be late for the service. I entered the chapel and found it dark and mostly empty. I picked up a bulletin, sat down in a pew and within a few minutes the pastor and assistants started walking down the center aisle, towards the altar, carrying a cross. It's fun exploring new religions, seeing their different traditions, garb and rituals. The pastor began with a prayer and some announcements. I didn't know if I was going to like the service.

The assistant then began to read the gospel and I began to get antsy. I felt like leaving. Oh come on, don't leave, I said to myself. The assistant finished the reading and the pastor walked up to the pulpit to begin his sermon.

If I'm going to leave, this would be a good time. I am really bored. Don't leave, I again said to myself, not every sermon is exciting and not every sermon has a message for you. Thirty seconds after my thought the pastor began his sermon by saying, *"The essence of faith is giving. There was a program on Cable T.V. about John D. Rockefeller, a man of great wealth, owning Standard Oil that supplied the oil for the whole country, but he was also a greedy man who was despised by the public. He did, however have a son, John Jr. who was a philanthropist who gave away the family fortune to charity and restored the public's opinion of the Rockefeller family...*

Oh, My God. That's the story I told Robert on our third

date! Why is this happening to me? I'm getting *Zapped* again!

This was the first time I went to this church. That program was on Cable T.V. about three months ago. It was an obscure program and just as I thought there would be no message for me in the sermon, he began telling the same story I had told Robert. What was happening to me?

I'm scared, I thought, as I began to weep quietly.

I got home and my father was not there, he was at St. Bernard's, which is where I should have gone! I probably wouldn't have been spooked there. With tears still in my eyes, I called my sister, Janice, who lived in Hicksville, ten minutes from my dad's house. "Hello, Janice? Something weird happened to me again!" and I began telling her about the strange coincidence.

"Oh it's just a coincidence."

"JUST A COINCIDENCE? There have been about twenty of these very bizarre, uncanny coincidences. It's creepy. I just have to stop praying, that's it. No, I don't want to stop praying. "

"You're just making a big deal about these coincidences."

"Well then why don't you try it? We'll do a control study. You say the rosary for sixty days and see if anything happens to you."

"Noooooooooooooooo, I'm happy here in Hicksville!!" she answered in a panic-stricken voice.

"I'm telling you Janice, this is spooky. I have an appointment with a psychiatrist this week."

"Good ask him what it is."

"I will, but I don't see how he will have any answers.

These are things that are happening out of my control. I should make an appointment to see Reverend Allison too."

"That's a good idea. Just try to calm down and I'll talk to you next week."

I hung up the phone, and a few minutes later my father walked in the door, returning from church. "Dad, there was another coincidence that just occurred."

"What happened?"

"Sit down and I'll tell you."

He sat on the couch and I began to tell him of the latest strange coincidence. When I finished telling him, he stared out into space and said softly, "If you had gone to St. Bernard's with me you never would have heard that. He then got up off the couch, with a fearful look on his face, pushed my arm, and said, "You have ghosts around you!" Then he walked into the kitchen.

I got up, followed him and asked, "Are you mad at me? I didn't do anything? What do you think the coincidences mean?"

"I don't know what they mean!" he replied still seeming very upset.

Well, I'm going to make an appointment to see the reverend at my church in Greenwich."

"Good, maybe he can figure it out."

Wednesday couldn't come fast enough as I eagerly awaited my appointment with Dr. Harill. As the day at the office progressed, I decided to give Robert a call to find out what his story was. Besides, I would need the information to tell the Shrink. I was nervous about calling Robert and kept putting it off until I couldn't wait any longer. It was a quarter to five when I finally called. I wasn't going to get upset. I was going to remain calm and hear what he had to say. I dialed the number and with each digit my heart pounded a little a faster. "Hello, Robert, how are you?"

"I'm okay. Well, I guess you're ready to beat me up, yell and scream at me."

"No, I'm not going to do anything you would expect me to do."

"That scares me even more."

"So, are you living with someone?" I asked calmly.

"Yes."

"How long have you been living with her?"

"Two years."

"Do you love her?"

"I can't say that."

"Do you love me?"

"I can't say that."

"Are you going to stay with her?"

"We've been through a lot and I don't want to hurt anybody."

"You know I went to a bookstore last week because I thought you had a fear of commitment and I picked up a book on the subject."

"I do have that problem," he quietly responded.

"Well as I read the book's description of a person who has a fear of commitment I said to myself, Yep, that sounds like Robert, but as I read on it sounded like me, too! It described me to a "T" and, I've decided to go to a shrink. Thanks to you, I'm starting to solve my problems."

"That's pretty brave of you."

Changing the subject I asked, "By the way, did you get my letter?"

"No, I haven't gotten it."

"You had to have gotten it! I mailed it over a week ago," I said, thinking he is so full of shit.

"Well let me see, I've got my mail on my desk now, maybe it's here. Look, I have some mail from Europe."

"You do business in Europe?"

"Oh, yeah, world-wide."

"Wow."

"This letter has flowers on it, maybe it's yours. Oh my God, oh my God!" Robert started shrieking over the phone.

"What Happened Robert?"

"There are stars coming out of this letter, just like the stars in your care package! I have your stars, now I have her stars!" he said with sheer terror in his voice.

"Who sent you that letter?

"Some woman from Holland!"

"That's freaky. Well, anyway I'm running late. I've got to go to the shrink now."

"Take me with you, and maybe I'll turn into a little man," Robert cried out. I can't believe this, he sounds like Gulliver again.

"Well I've got to go, talk to you soon," I said hanging up the phone feeling a little freaked out by what had just transpired. I grabbed my coat and bag and headed for the front door.

I hailed a cab uptown and arrived at Dr. Harill's office on time. I walked into the small, but pleasant waiting area, grabbed a magazine, sat down and began to read. As I waited for the doctor, I could hear there was another patient in the office finishing up the session. A few minutes later the patient emerged from the office. A few seconds after that, a tall, pleasant looking man, with a mustache and a friendly smile, who was about 40 years old came out and introduced himself. He led me into his office.

I sat down on the proverbial couch and began talking. I decided to lay my cards on the table and tell him everything beginning with my family history. I told him about my mother's alcoholism, my suicide attempt, and my lousy track record with men. Then finally I began to tell him about Robert, and the bizarre coincidences. I only had forty-five minutes and I wanted to get the whole basic story in at the first session.

Each time I recounted another coincidence, the doctor either sat in his chair shaking his head, widening his eyes, or just uttering "Hmm," seemingly amazed. When I finally finished telling him the sequence of events with the last co-incidence of the stars flying out of the letter, I asked him, "Now what is it?"

"I don't know. It's a series of coincidences," he replied looking baffled.

"Well, I've made an appointment to see a reverend to-morrow night."

"I'll be very interested to hear what the reverend has to say."

The next evening I caught the 5:10 train out of the city so I would make my six o'clock appointment with Reverend Allison. I stopped at the local Starbuck's, picked up two cafe lattes and a cinnamon scone. It would be nice to bring a little something to munch on; a good icebreaker.

I'd been going to Second Congregational Church almost every Sunday looking for the Reverend who *Zapped* me with his sermon, *Being Afraid to Love*. I discovered his name was Tom Murphy. He was the associate minister at Second Con-gregational. He was filling in for Reverend Allison on that particular Sunday. And he'd been reading the Gospel at every Sunday service since. I just hadn't recognized him without his vestments on!

But the services with Reverend Allison have been fabulous. He's a wonderful guy; funny as all hell. He looks like Santa Claus with his white hair and beard and his happy, giving spirit always makes you feel good.

Ron, as he prefers to be called, uses no notes in presenting his sermons. He seldom stands at the pulpit. As he talks, he moves around the alter platform with a cordless microphone attached to his vestment. He walks part way or all the way down the platform steps to stand before congregants in the front pews, speaking at times softly or rising in tone or pitch as he makes a strong point.

Allison enlivens his sermons with personal anecdotes related to Bible passages. He brings the Gospel into modern day life. He once began his sermon by saying, "I put on my Sears Roebuck suit and went down there in my red pickup truck." Then he would go off on a tangent and said, "I often wonder what it would be like to drive off in a Porsche. That would be really neat." But he's so unpretentious and down to earth. It's the red Chevy pickup that personifies Ron's personality.

His Valentine's Day sermon is one that really stands out in my mind. Among his dramatic effects was doing an imitation of Elvis Presley, singing "Love me Tender" with accompanying gyrations as part of the act. It was hilarious.

And his sermon on Snow White when he sat down on the front steps of the altar and asked the children in the congregation to come up and join him. They were so precious. He began by saying, "Now, Snow White was from Greenwich, Connecticut." He is so funny.

He often uses family members—what they have done or said—to illustrate a point in his sermons. He also frequently relates to us his encounters with people, old and young, at the Grand Union supermarket near his home. And several times he has told us about a homeless man he invited into the London church he previously served.

Members of the congregation are included by name in sermons when Ron, usually humorously, tells something about them or directly asks, "What would you do in this situation?"

It was very entertaining going to Second Congregational Church. Never a dull moment, and when you leave the service, Reverend Allison always gave you a big hug. I remember one parishioner even had pins made up saying "I got my hug today." She handed them out at the coffee hour they have after services. You always got a laugh and a hug with Ron.

I entered the church office and was greeted very warmly by my favorite Rev. I sat down on the wing chair in the corner, started to take the coffees out of the bag. I was a little nervous. This was the first time I really sat down to talk with him.

"I've brought us some coffee and cake. I hope you like cafe lattes," I said feeling a little shaky.

"I do and I can see you are a very generous person."

"Why doesn't everyone who comes to see you do something like this?"

"Yeah, right," he said letting out a chuckle.

"Well, I've come to you for two reasons. First I would like

to officially join the church but, secondly, I've had a very strange experience I'd like to discuss with you."

"Why don't we start by you giving me a little background on yourself? Tell me where you were born, your family history, what you do for a living and so on and so forth."

"Okay," I said and began giving him the same low-down as I gave the shrink, my complete neurotic background and any information about myself that I felt might be relevant. I revealed the coincidences to him one-by-one and he reacted differently each time, but his reactions were similar to the shrink's. Sometimes he look amazed, sometimes he would chuckle, and sometimes he would look up at the ceiling, smile and shake his head. He was definitely enjoying the story and when I finally finished I sat back with a slightly frightened look on my face and said, "Now, what is it?"

He looked at me, smiled, and said, "Why it's providence."

"What's providence?" I asked with a puzzled look on my face.

"Why it's God trying to tell you something. It's Divine Guidance."

"But, it scares me,"

"Why does it scare you?"

"I'm always anxious, never knowing when the next coincidence will happen. I've even tried to predict when one will happen, but I can't do that. I don't know, it's just spooky. Do you know anyone else that this has happened to?"

"Yes, I know a few people that this has happened to. I dont want you to be scared by them. Just let them happen and you decide what message is for you."

"How do you explain these coincidences?" I asked.

"I believe they're the power of the Holy Spirit," he said.

"I think they're angels or spirit guides that whisper in our ears, giving us suggestions, guidance and direction that in turn create the coincidence." I replied.

"Yes. That could be it. There's a lot to think about."

But, what you have to do now, Marianne, is go out and find yourself. Find out what Marianne Thompson is all about."

"But, what about Robert?" I asked hoping for a positive response.

"What about Robert? He deceived you."

"Is there any hope for us?"

"Yes, there's hope, but it has to happen now. No more waiting. No more stringing you along. It's funny though that you both have the same problem."

"We could solve our problems together," I said with tears streaming down my cheeks.

"Maybe you will be able to solve your problems together. This could be an opportunity for Robert."

I then turned to him and said, "This is a good story isn't it? These coincidences are uncanny. I should write a book. I have to write a book, I really, really, really have to write a book."

"Yes, this is a good story and you should write a book. Let's have some fun, Marianne. I'd like to give you a personality test," He said as he walked over to his bookcase and selected a paperback from the second shelf. "This is the Keirsey-Bates personality test entitled, *Please Understand Me*. It's widely used by therapists and I use it a lot in my marriage counseling. I'd like you to go home, take the test, and we'll go over the results the next time you come in. We can have some fun with this test."

"Alright, I'll take it and, I'd also like to get together in a couple of weeks."

"That's fine, just give me a call at the office to set up an appointment."

"Thanks for everything, Reverend Allison." I got up, and he walked me out to the hall and said, "Take care, Marianne. Nice to see you." Then he bent over and gave me one of his famous hugs. You always felt happy after you saw Reverend Allison. He is a rare and wonderful man.

I got into my car and headed toward the Greenwich Public Library, to take out some psychology books and try to solve some of my problems. I walked in and headed for the computers and punched in the subject matter. I then walked to the psychology section looking for the books I had selected. In my search I stumbled upon a book entitled, *Man's Search for Himself* written by Rollo May. The title of the book intrigued me because the Rev had told me I had to find myself. I picked it up, deciding to take it home with my other selections.

Shortly after arriving home, I made myself a little snack, lay down on the couch and began to read *Man's Search For Himself*. Rollo May's theory is that our problems in adulthood stem from unresolved childhood conflicts, many times, concerning the parent you so loved. My dad? This was very upsetting to me because I was very close to my dad when I was a little girl. These unresolved childhood conflicts are usually linked to the traumatic events in one's life. Hmm, I can't figure out what unresolved childhood conflicts I have with my dad. I always thought my Mom's alcoholism was the root of all my problems.

I continued reading for another hour when I decided to stop and take that personality test the Reverend Allison had given me. It was filled with day–to-day living questions concerning how you would react to certain situations and personal philosophy questions.

I answered the questions in each section, tallied up my score and I was totally shocked when my personality came under the heading of *The Author*! It says I should be an Author! I just got done telling Reverend Allison how I had to write a book on all these strange coincidences.

A day or two later, I remembered my sister's boyfriend had given me the same test about five years prior. And the results were the same with my personality again coming under the heading of *The Author*. At that time my sister said, "It's funny because, every time something major occurs in your life or when you are exasperated with a situation, you always say, 'I should write a book...I have to write a book.' So why don't you write a book?" she asked. So, I started one on the Fashion Industry, but I didn't have the confidence to go forward. Another time I wanted to write a book on the dating scene, but never thought it was possible. Me, a writer? Who was I kidding?

All along, people have told me that I have a flair with the written word. After arguments with friends or family I would sit down and write very philosophical, moral letters and people always complimented me on my letter writing. Friends urged me to go on with the book I had started on the Fashion Industry, but my self-esteem just wouldn't allow it. Now I discover it really is in my personality.

An Author. Wow!

YOUR CHEATIN' HEART

It was a Saturday afternoon and I was attempting to hang the beautiful new living room drapes my sample hand Maria had made for me. A difficult task to do by yourself and the scene was one out of I Love Lucy as I stood on the ladder, attaching one end of the valence into the bracket on the wall, dragging the ladder over to the other side, tried to attach the other side into the bracket when the first side fell down. I gave it another shot, but to no avail with the results ending in the same frustrating comical scene: me wavering on the ladder, rods flying every which way, curtains falling as I finally let out my Lucy wail.

Exasperated, I went and knocked on my neighbor Deb's door to ask if she could give me a hand. She said she would be over in a little while after she got off the phone. I went back to make myself a cool drink, sat down in my favorite chair and decided to relax for a while.

A few minutes latter the doorbell rang. I got up to answer it expecting to greet my neighbor, but was surprised to see Patti and Annie standing there. Annie was another friend of mine from the Brett's crowd.

"Well, what a surprise. Why are you here?

"Annie and I have to tell you something."

A sense of dread washed over me as I invited them in and wondered what they were going to say.

"You'd better sit down for this one," Patti said.

"God, what is it? You're scaring me. Come, let's sit in the living room. As you can see I've been trying to hang my drapes. My neighbor was supposed to help, but perhaps you can, after we have our little talk. Let me get you something to drink first." I went into the kitchen, poured two diet cokes, and came back to the living room in jitters. "Now what have you to tell me?"

Patti looked at me very seriously with very sad eyes and said, "Annie has a friend, Karen, who was also going out with Robert Brenner at the same time you were."

Annie then said, "That's right. I was talking to my friend the other day and she told me about this guy Robert she used to date who owned Omega Sound, and then I told her I think it's the same guy Marianne's dating. Maybe you should talk to her. I could call her right now if you'd like. She's really nice, she'll tell you what happened."

I was numb as I sat there in disbelief with mouth dropped open. "He was dating me and another girl at the same time he's living with someone else? I can't believe this. Yes, let's call Karen right now."

Annie called Karen and said, "Hi, it's me. I'm over here at Marianne's, the girl that was also dating Robert Brenner and she'd like to talk to you. Okay, here she is." Nervously I took the phone and introduced myself.

"So, when were you dating Robert?" I asked.

"End of June into July."

"That's the same time I was dating him. Did you know that he was living with someone?" I asked.

"When I met Robert, he told me he was living with someone but that it was over and she was supposed to move out in August. When I hadn't heard from him for a while and was getting pissed, I called his live in. Her name is Paula. I told her I was dating Robert and asked her if it was true that she was planning to move out in August. She told me she wasn't going anywhere and that this wasn't the first time she had this problem with him. She went on to say that she is engaged to Robert and has been living with him for twelve years!

Twice they had made all the plans for their wedding; hall booked, everything paid for; and twice he backed out at the last minute saying he couldn't go through with the wedding. Then she said to me, 'I want to confront him. Come on over.' So, I went over to their home. She called Robert at the office and told him 'An old college buddy of yours just dropped in, come on home.'

Robert came home only to see me sitting in the kitchen with Paula. He was in shock when he saw me. Then he asked Paula, 'Is this really your college buddy?' At that point I started to scream at him, 'How could you do this?' He went upstairs to the bedroom. We both followed him up. Then I slapped him across the face. Then Paula started hitting him. It was a real scene. That guy was such a liar, I didn't have anything to do with him after that."

"This is unbelievable. Back in July he told me an old college buddy of his dropped in to see him, but he used it as an excuse why he couldn't see me one weekend. I can't believe this. Did you ever sleep with him?" I asked.

"Just once," she replied.

"He told me that we should wait, but we did have sex; also just once. Did he tell you he loved you?"

"No." Her tone of voice was filled with such anger throughout the entire conversation, she was almost screaming in my ear.

"You sound so angry. Try to put your anger aside. The man is sick. He needs help."

"I don't give a shit about that fucking asshole after what he did to me!"

So much for putting anger aside. "Well, thanks for telling me this. I'll give you back to Annie now." I handed Annie the phone and sat there dumbfounded.

"I'm sorry we had to tell you this Marianne," Patti said.

"What a story! His live-in is just as sick as he is. 'This isn't the first time I've had this problem with Robert and I'm not going anywhere.' Do you believe that? He doesn't love her. How could he? But, he's trapped because anytime he meets someone he cares about he's too frightened to go forward. I feel sorry for Robert. He's sick. He really needs to see a psychiatrist. He has to get help."

"I know, he really is screwed up."

"It's sad, because he only does these things because of his problems. I don't want to go out with him anymore, but he really needs to get help."

"Yes, but it's not your problem," Patti said.

"I don't want to talk about it anymore. Do you want to help me hang my drapes?" We got up and it took only a few minutes to get the drapes up and looking beautiful. Then we all decided to go to Thataway's Cafe at the bottom of Greenwich Avenue, for a late afternoon snack.

A few days had gone by and I still thought about Robert. I couldn't put him out of my mind. I was angry at his deceiving me, and there was no way I would go out with him again, but at the same time I still cared about him. It was Thursday night; the big night at Brett's, and I bet he'd be there. Patti was supposed to meet me there at seven-thirty; I started to get ready.

Nervously I walked into a packed Brett's. Patti was standing at the middle of the bar. I made my way through the crowd and she greeted me warmly.

"Robert's here. He came over before to ask if you were going to be here tonight. I told him that Annie informed us he was also going out with Karen at the same time he was going out with you. I then told him he was sick. That he was worse than a two-timer, he was a three-timer. I told him he needed help."

"What did he say?"

"He looked at me funny."

"Where is he?"

"He's over there at the end of the bar."

I looked over, he saw me, and acknowledged me by raising his glass and mouthing hello. I took two big gulps of my drink to calm my nerves and said to Patti, "I'm going over there to talk to Robert." I squeezed through the crowd as the band was playing and a minute later I greeted him. "Hi, how are you?"

"I'm okay, I guess."

"I hear you had a talk with Annie."

"Listen, I don't like Karen, I like you."

"But, you're living with someone, Robert, and I discovered you forgot to put a one in front of the two when you told me how long you've been living with your girlfriend. You've been living with her for twelve years, not two. Why did you lie?"

Robert turned his head away, stared out in front of him and said, "I don't know." Then he started talking in tangents. "I know why I can't marry you or Karen. It's because I don't believe in divorce."

"What about Paula? Why don't you marry Paula, Robert?"

Again, he stared out into space and said, "I don't know?" And again, he continued with these tangents, as he obviously had a few drinks in him. "You see, I like people. It's like I go from land to land."

This is bizarre. He sounds like Gulliver again. I never told him about the Gulliver's Travels coincidence. "Robert, did you ever read Gulliver's Travels?"

His face came alive. He slammed his drink on the bar and exclaimed, "THAT'S IT! I'M GULLIVER!" When I heard this I couldn't help but crack up laughing.

"Robert, I want to tell you my story about all these strange coincidences that have been happening to me."

He looked frightened as he said, "No, I don't want to hear about it. I don't care."

"Well, I'm going back to my friends."

"You're so beautiful", he said, touching my face, "Your hair, your skin, and the pretty dress you have on. Do you want to smooch?"

"No, I don't want to smooch, and you've had too much to drink." I walked back to Patti thinking he is so neurotic. I stayed a little while longer, but my spirit was down so I decided to call it a night. I walked back to my apartment feeling tired and numb. Thank God, I have an appointment with my therapist, Dr. Harill, tomorrow. Perfect timing.

The day dragged at the office and I was still obsessed with Robert. I knew it was ridiculous, but I just couldn't stop thinking about him.

It was a welcome moment to enter Dr. Harill's office. I waited a few minutes in the reception area, and then was warmly greeted by him. I finally sat down and began to tell the doctor of the latest events unfolding with Robert. "Marianne, I know it's going to be hard, but you're going to have to forget about Robert."

"Forget about Robert! How can I with all the coincidences? He just needs to get help. We could solve our problems together."

"You're sounding awfully co-dependent."

"What does co-dependent mean?"

"It means you want to rescue Robert."

"That's me," I said with a smile, raising both arms with clenched fists and giving the co-dependent cheer. "Co-dependent, Co-dependent, Co-dependent," I giggled as I put my hands down and the doctor shook his head at me. "I once read that adult children of alcoholics are sometimes co-dependent."

"That's right, they have the rescue syndrome. Co-dependents are so focused and preoccupied with the needs, behaviors and problems of the important people in their lives that they neglect themselves."

"But, Robert really should go into therapy."

"You can't control other people's behavior. When you hear yourself saying, 'He should do this' or 'he shouldn't have done that.' When you hear the word 'should' coming out of your mouth that means you're trying to control someone's behavior. People do what they want to do, not what you think they should do. When you first start dating someone you should just be observing his behaviors, not trying to control him. But for now we have to concentrate on your problems, Marianne. You can't help Robert, only he can help himself."

"Alright, I'll forget about him for the moment. I'd like to talk about that blocked memory that came back to me with the uncontrollable screaming. What was that all about?"

"Those are called night terrors. There have been studies done on people who have grown up in alcoholic homes and who have experiences similar to those of men coming back from war. It's called Post-Traumatic Stress Syndrome. The result is a cluster of symptoms such as feelings of insecurity, depression and sadness. These symptoms may appear *long after* the initial trauma and can last for years and into your lifetime. The blocked memories coming back are like flashbacks. The traumatic event of the past was triggered and brought back the feelings associated with it."

"That was a really scary experience when that blocked memory came to the surface. It was horrifying."

"You actually re-experienced the trauma and pain. The uncontrollable screams you experienced was a release of energy that had built up to a level of chronic distress. In order to undo the damage and find what was lost, we have to go back to the scene of the crime, to the place where we were wounded. The blocked memory you experienced is a perfect example of that. Your anxiety level dropped considerably after that experience didn't it?" he asked.

"Tremendously. Even though it was a nightmare to re-experience the event."

I looked down and sat quietly for a minute with an intense feeling of emptiness and sadness. I felt totally gypped growing up in an alcoholic home. I often felt as if I never had a mother. Not a real one. And that's something I'll never get back. There's a tremendous void in my life.

I was trying very hard not to cry when Dr. Harill said to me, "You're not alone Marianne. Most homes are dysfunctional in some way. In your family it was alcoholism, in mine it was rage."

"Oh God, it was horrible growing up in an alcoholic home, especially when my father was away on business.

"I remember one summer evening, I must have been around nine, coming home from a friend's at about seventhirty only to find my mother sitting on the grass in the front yard, in a drunken stupor, playing with the dog. As I approached her, the only thing she had to say was 'Go to bed.' 'But, mommy, none of the other kids have to go to bed so early. It's summertime, there's no school.' She looked up at me with glazed eyes and said, *'I told you to go to bed!'* I ran into the house crying and went upstairs to my bedroom. I sat on my bed and began to look out of the window. The kid next door was outside playing and when he looked up and saw me at the window he yelled up, 'Ha, Ha, Ha your mother's a drunk.' I quickly turned from the window, and burst out crying. Why did I have to have an alcoholic mom? I cried and cried drenching my pillow with tears.

"It was wrong of my father to leave small children in the care of an alcoholic mother!" I cried out to Dr. Harill as I pounded my fist on the arm of the couch. He handed me a tissue and I wiped the tears from my eyes.

"You know, I never used to think he did anything wrong. I always thought he had to leave us, because he had to go to work, he was a traveling salesman. But, no! It was wrong! He should have gotten another job. It was dangerous to leave his children in the care of an alcoholic mother. How could he have done that?"

"He was in denial, Marianne."

"God, I hated it when he went away on business. I think I have a fear of abandonment because of it."

"You're probably right about that. Fear of abandonment has to do with the issue of trust and is often exaggerated in children who grew up in dysfunctional families. Also the inconsistency of the parent-child relationship where we feel loved one day and rejected the next is another reason behind this terrible fear of abandonment. So what usually happens in your relationships?"

"Whenever I feel that a man I'm dating is pulling away, I start pursuing him and then it ends, but these guys are usually emotionally unavailable; they all seem to have a fear of commitment. My relationships never last more that six months and usually only two to three months. Then I pine over them. There was a guy I pined over for two years and I only dated him for three months! During the time we dated he was always busy, only able to see me every other weekend, and after the breakup I didn't date for two years! Why do I behave this way? Why? Why? Why?"

"This is going to take time. We'll find out why, but for now we're going to have to stop and continue this next time."

I always hate it when the shrink cuts off the session. It seems so unnatural, but I guess that's the way it has to be. I thought that was a pretty good session. Little by little I'll solve my problems.

I boarded the train, found a window seat, and decided I was going to finish reading *Gulliver's Travels* since remnants of Gulliver seem to be popping up all over the place. Jonathan Swift's book is a wonderful adventure story and I can't help but think there might be some kind of message there for me.

Lemuel Gulliver was born to a family of modest means in Nottinghamshire, England. He was fortunate enough to have been able to complete an education in medicine and, subsequently became a ship's doctor. A series of shipwrecks, piracies, and storms caused his ship to go off course, bringing Gulliver to many different lands. Very strange lands, indeed.

The first one was Lilliput where Gulliver was a giant who was held captive by men no more than six inches tall. It was a land where everything was one-twelfth of normal size.

Two months later, Gulliver began a second voyage where his ship was blown way off course by strong winds. The ship reached Brobdingnaga, land of giants, where this time everything was twelve times larger than normal size.

Gulliver's last voyage is my favorite. Gulliver wound up in the Land of the Houyhnhnm. The Houyhnhnms were super rational horses, innocent and uncorrupted. They were reasonable and truthful. Also on this island live the Yahoo's. They were filthy, hairy beasts that walked on their hind legs like humans. The Yahoos represented mankind depraved. Swift positioned Gulliver mid-way between the super rational, innocent horses and the filthy, depraved Yahoos. But because of his physical shape, the horses compared Gulliver to a Yahoo. Gulliver was horrified and his pride led him to try to become a horse.

Gulliver learned quickly the language of the Houyhnhnm and before long, he was teaching the horses about English life. He talked at length about wars fought for "religious reasons." The horses were shocked and thought that the European Yahoos were far worse than the Yahoos in the

Land of the Houyhnhnm for they used their reason to magnify, yet excuse, their vices. Gulliver then taught the Houyhnhnm's about lying and they were astonished by the notion of a "lie" and could not understand the concept of why people would want to misrepresent themselves.

As I read the last few pages of Gulliver's Travels, I was saddened that the ending had come so soon. The book marvelously illustrated all the different variations of human nature. The book was written so long ago. It was published in 1726, two hundred and sixty years ago.

Man hasn't changed a bit. Gulliver was portrayed at times as, "gullible" and naive. Sounds a little like me.

It also seemed since Gulliver left his family and traveled from "land to land" he might have had a fear of intimacy or a fear of commitment. The book also demonstrated how pride gets in the way of Gulliver's reason on many occasions. I guess there's a little bit of Gulliver in all of us, but Robert Brenner definitely sounds like a Yahoo to me!

BACK ON THE COUCH

The week flew by. As I walked up Seventh Avenue to Dr. Harill's office, I was eager to get to my next session. This was the first time in my life I really wanted to go into therapy. Believe it or not, I didn't even want to go when I was suicidal. I went, but I didn't want to be there. I continued my weekly sessions with Dr. Harill and I had bi-weekly sessions with Reverend Allison.

Dr. Harill took care of my head; Reverend Allison took care of the *Zappings* as well as my head. I was covered on all bases. I used to be ashamed of going into therapy, which probably stemmed from my Irish Catholic background. The Irish aren't big on therapy. Their therapy consists of brushing everything under the carpet. Repression at it's best. I remember when I was suicidal my older sister told me to "Just snap out of it."

My father had a unique way of trying to cheer me up after he found out I was contemplating suicide. I decided to go home for a while and when he picked me up at the railroad station, he greeted me in one of those funny joke glasses with the nose and mustache attached to it. Needless to say, that didn't go over too well. He couldn't deal with the reality of the situation.

As I walked into my session with Dr. Harill I realized I had forgotten my checkbook. "You're not going to believe this, idiot that I am, I forgot my checkbook." I said to him feeling rather foolish. "Don't worry about it Marianne, you can pay me next time." After a few minutes of conversation, he said to me, "I get the feeling that you don't think you're very smart."

"Why, what makes you say that?"

"Certain things you say."

"Like what?"

"On many occasions when we are discussing issues, you use self-deprecating language."

"Oh, you mean when I just said, 'Idiot that I am'?"

"Yes, you say things like that all the time."

"You're right, I don't think I'm very smart. I never did very well in school. I was always told I was capable but I didn't apply myself. And, I never gave myself a break. Never considering that my grades might have been different if I hadn't been living in the turmoil of an alcoholic home."

"Well you've got to start building up your self-esteem by cutting out the self-deprecating language. That's not good."

Then we talked about Robert and how I just couldn't stop thinking about him.

"Why am I so obsessed with Robert? I wish I could just forget about him. I'm so infatuated with him."

"This is a limited way of experiencing love, as that of 'fa ling in love'."

"But there was so much chemistry between us," I said

"You seem to be caught up in the "chemistry" of romantic love. When we get beyond these lower stages of love, we are able to see the other person realistically. The relationship is not based on fantasy, but rather on honesty, trust, and compatibility. In a healthy relationship we are able to talk freely about the issues that are important to the relationship. We have empathy, respect and compassion for our partners as they do for us. In a healthy relationship, we make a commitment to our own and our partners, total growth, physically, emotionally and spiritually. My ultimate goal is to get you into a healthy relationship and to experience love on a deeper level."

The rest of the session flew by as usual.

A week later, I was in the basement doing my laundry. Our laundry room is different from most because it has a library in it, consisting of old books donated by the tenants.

I set my laundry bag down and moseyed over to see if there was anything interesting on the bookshelves. I didn't see anything I liked but kept digging and came up with a meditation book. Rollo May was a proponent of meditation as a form of prayer and a way of getting closer to God. This book happened to be a religious book with 40 guided imagery meditations for personal prayer. It interested me so, I brought it back to the apartment.

Later that evening, I began reading different meditations when I got to this one:

In your imagination, go to a classroom,
one that you remember...

Pretend to be the teacher for a while:
Fill the classroom with all the people
you would like to give advice to--
especially those, this year,
whom you'd like to tell off...
or tell them to grow up!....

Give them a good lecturing...
Enjoy this pose for a while.
Now change roles...
You become the student...

Get out a sheet of paper from the desk
and start taking dictation...

You have a number of "teachers" up in front of the room.
They are some of the people who, now and then, have given
you advice.

Recall the criticisms and complaints against yourself, which
you have received--especially most recently...

I began to feel very uncomfortable with this part of the meditation, when all of a sudden in my mind's eye I had a picture of me as a seven-year-old sitting in my second grade class with my head down, forefinger in my mouth looking very, very sad.

"Why are you so sad?" I asked this vision of myself, wanting to draw out the thoughts of that sad little girl sitting in the classroom.

"I took a test and I got a "C" on it," the little girl answered, head down, fidgeting in her chair. "Well, that's not so bad," I said, trying to comfort that little girl. "What did your teacher say?" I asked.

"My teacher told me to have my mommy help me." 'So, why do you look so sad?' 'I asked my mommy to help me, but she said, 'No, you have to do it yourself.' I did it myself and I got a "C", I'm stupid."

I put down the book and started breathing quickly, heart pounding, OH MY GOD, IT'S HAPPENING AGAIN. SCREAMS OF TERROR ARE POURING OUT OF ME! HOW COULD SHE HAVE DONE THAT? I WAS JUST A BABY! SHE SHOULD HAVE HELPED ME! SHE SHOULD HAVE HELPED ME!

I caught my breath for a minute and then my mind flashed forward *twenty* years to The Fashion Institute of Technology. I was in my draping class, with a jacket I had draped on the dress form. I needed help with my sleeve because it wasn't hanging right. I called the teacher over and asked her for help. She turned to me and said, "No, you have to do it yourself."

I flipped out, ran out into the hallway and my friend followed me. "She should help me, she should help me!! I'm paying her salary!" "Marianne, you know more than you think you know." My friend answered, because she was aware of all the insecurities I had about my work.

I NEVER THOUGHT I WAS GOOD ENOUGH! I once again had to put my pillow to my face, for my screams were uncontrollable!

I finally calmed down after about half an hour, laid back and quietly cried. God, it's amazing how things that happened when I was seven wind up years later in a classroom at the Fashion Institute. At the time, I didn't realize my over-reaction was related to what happened to me in second grade. Traumatic events from the past are linked to our futures. Unresolved childhood conflicts, repressed, and thrown up twenty years later.

My heart broke for that sad little girl with the red hair. It just wasn't fair.

In my next session with Dr. Harill, I sat on the couch, crying uncontrollably as I told him of my latest blocked memory coming back. "WHAT COULD I HAVE BEEN?" I screamed, pounding my fist on the arm of the chair. What could I have done with my life if I had the proper love and care as a child? God, I remember once when I had to select my major in high school. My mother and I were in the office of the guidance counselor and when I was asked what I wanted to be, I replied, 'A Garbage Man!' Why wasn't the school psychologist brought in? How much more evident could my lack of self-esteem be? What could I have been?"

"I don't know Marianne. When a child is older, it's okay to encourage them to be independent with their schoolwork. But, certainly not at the age of seven. That was wrong, Marianne."

I was at a loss for words.

He then said, "Marianne, I know that was very painful for you. In the long run you'll feel better getting this all out. You're dealing with unresolved grief concerning a traumatic event in your life. After experiencing a trauma, energy builds up within us. This energy needs to be released. When we do not grieve in a complete and healthy way, it has a debilitating effect on our emotional and physical well-being. Your tears and your screams are a release of this energy. After so many years you are finally thoroughly grieving for what had happened to you as a child."

"Sounds like unresolved grief might have something to do with repression. I have a tendency to repress things."

"As a child were you given the negative message of *don't talk about it?*"

"Definitely. Almost every night was pure chaos when I was growing up. My mother was falling down drunk, but the next morning nothing was ever said. We ate our breakfast in silence. Nothing was ever discussed."

"You were not allowed to grieve your losses completely. You repressed your feelings. These rules and patterns of repressing anger and hurt are *carried into adulthood.* So, when someone hurts you don't say anything. But the problems just don't go away. They get stuffed deep inside and then they come out later in disguised ways. Perhaps you will over-react to a totally unrelated issue, when in actuality, it is the unresolved grief that was triggered. For example, like the woman at your office who said something cruel to you and you wound up crying for half the day. You over-reacted because *unconsciously* she reminded you of your mother."

I got home that evening and called my friend, Janet, who I don't get to see that often since she now lives in Florida. I've been a friend of Janet's since I was 13. God, that's 27 years. Nobody knows me better except my family. I've been calling her regularly throughout this whole ordeal and my phone bill is out of control.

"Hi, Janet, it's me, Marianne. Just got back from my shrink. I had another blocked memory come back." I said and gave her the details.

"Did you ever take child psychology in school?"

"Yeah, but I don't remember much about it."

"Well, seven is the age of autonomy. It's the age where you form opinions about yourself."

"That's horrible, and it's just not fair."

"No, it's not. But, you'll get through this. Whatever happened with Robert?"

"Well, I'll have to give you the details on that front, too. He's been living with someone, for twelve years not two. I just wish he'd break up with her and get help."

"Boy, you really know how to pick them. Forget about Robert."

"I can't. I'm totally obsessed. Hey, will you read me my Tarot Cards?" She dabbles in the occult so, I'm always bugging her to read my cards.

"Okay, what question do you want to ask?"

"Is Robert Brenner going to break up with Paula?"

"Okay, we'll have that answer in a minute, I'm shuffling the cards, placing them in the proper order. Now let's see, what do we have here. That relationship was over a long time ago. Yep, he's going to break up with her. All these cards are very positive."

"Really? Do you really think so?"

"Yep, it's in the cards."

"Oh Goodie. Well, I'm going to let you go now. As always, it was great talking to you. Talk to you soon. Okay, bye."

I got off the phone and I couldn't stop thinking about Robert. I have some things to tell him. I know I probably shouldn't do this, but I don't care. I'm going to write him another letter. I sat back, and grinned as the brainstorm struck...

September 16, 1994

Dear Gulliver, (AKA King of the Dragon Slayers)

I am now leaving the Land of the Yahoo's where I have spent the first 40 years of my life. I am on my voyage to the land of the Houyhnhnms where I would like to spend the last half of my life. But, I had to make one last stop in the Land of Co-dependency.

For now, this will be the last letter I will write to you. Obviously, we can't have a relationship when you are still living with someone. I am still in shock about the nature of your relationship with this woman. You have been living with her for twelve years; two times you had all the plans made to get married but, you backed out both times. You have cheated on her numerous times. When I asked you if you loved her, you said you couldn't say that. She knows all this and she's not going anywhere. It's cruel to stay with a woman if you can't say you love her and have no plans to marry her. But, she seems to enjoy the abuse. Beat me!! Whip me!! And, you stay in a dead end relationship and deny yourself the love you deserve. This is a masochistic relation-ship and you need to address your problems.

About five months ago, I began to pray heavily and asked God to help me solve my problems. About six weeks after I started praying, I met you. Gee, thanks God, I asked you to help me solve my prob-lems, not increase them. But, I fell "head over heels." Then a series of bizarre coincidences began to hap-

*pen to me. The coincidences scared me so, I went to
a minister and asked, "What is it?" He said, "Why
it's Providence. God's trying to tell you something." I
don't know what this all means, but I am beginning
to solve my problems.*

*I have enclosed the book Man's Search for
Himself because it has helped me in many ways.
You are a brilliant man, Robert. Most men couldn't
even dream of what you have accomplished with
Omega Sound. But, your greatest accomplishment of
all should be the solving of your problems, for only
that will bring you true happiness.*

*Good Luck in your travels, Gulliver. Sometimes
the rough seas ahead will be scary, but I know you
can make it to the Land of the Houyhnhnms!*

Love,

Marianne

I got a kick out of writing that letter and I giggled as I
placed the letter inside the book and wrapped it in brown
paper, but I also hoped Robert would start to solve some of
his problems. God, I can't believe this guy. He's brilliant,
but why can't he look at his problems. Hey, wait a minute, I
just figured out something. Remember the question posed
by Jonathan Swift---A man has three faces, he looks in the
mirror and what does he see? And the answer was nothing.
That means he doesn't see his problems! Just like I didn't
see that I have a fear of commitment. I finally figured it out.
That's what it means.

I don't know what I want from Robert at this point. I know I can't have a relationship with him now while he's living with that girl, but somehow I hope he' gets his act together. In some way I still feel destined to be with him. All these coincidences. What do they mean?

SEARCH FOR ANSWERS

The doors of the subway opened and I pushed my way through the crowds, grabbed the handrail and wondered how I lived in the city for so many years or at least why I took the subway everyday.

I was squished in the car. The girl next to me had B.O.. A homeless man was panhandling down the aisle, and some creep across from me kept looking me up and down. Nothing like a restful repose after a hard day at the office. The things we adapt to in this city are unbelievable.

My only saving grace was that I only had three stops until I reached my destination, East 72nd Street. I climbed up from the black hole in the ground into a very quaint neighborhood on the East Side. Funny how the city is such a mixed bag of good and bad. I wandered up Lexington Avenue heading towards East 74th street, which was where my class was to be held.

I had decided to take a little diversion from my normal

therapy by signing up for an adult continuing education course featured in the Learning Annex. The course is entitled, *Overcoming your Fears and Phobias.* It was offered for one night only consisting of three hours. Therefore, I had to cram in as much as possible. This should be interesting, I thought as I opened the doors and followed the signs to the second floor.

The class was small and intimate, only about ten people, and the instructor was a balding, middle-aged man with a pleasant smile who was also a shrink in his day job. He greeted the class with a small introduction about what the course was about and then asked, "Would anyone like to start talking about their fears or phobias?"

I was the first one to raise my hand and that in itself amazed me because I was always pretty shy in group situations. "Yes, I would. I have a fear of abandonment and I'm attracted to men with a fear of commitment. I'd like to get married and this is getting me nowhere. I also think I have fear of commitment myself."

"Okay, now why do you think you have a fear of abandonment?"

"Because when I was a little girl, my father used to travel a lot on business and he left us in the care of my mom who was an alcoholic. This went on from about the time I was seven until the time I was twelve years old."

"Now what is the pattern in your relationships with men?"

"When I meet someone, I usually fall head over heels, but shortly afterwards when the man starts to pull away, I panic and I pursue him and he usually gets scared away."

"Well maybe the man isn't really going anywhere. You just expect he's going to leave and so you panic."

"I expect him to leave? I don't understand," I said feeling puzzled.

"There are two things going on here. What happened when your father went away on business?"

"I was very upset, I was very sad."

"But, you knew or expected that your father was going to leave. Now what happened when your father came back? There must have been a lot of excitement."

"Yes, that's right. He would always bring me souvenirs and gifts."

"So, when you meet these guys, there is a lot of excitement in the beginning, then you expect they are going to abandon you or unconsciously you even want them to abandon you, thus starting the whole cycle again. Your responses to these men are unconscious. They are Pavlovian responses. If you took any Psychology classes you learned that Pavlov was famous for his description of classical conditioning. He observed that his experimental subjects, dogs, came to salivate at the sound of a neutral stimulus--say a bell-- if food and bell were repeatedly paired together.

There is a cycle to your pattern. You meet a guy, and there's a lot of excitement in the beginning. Then you expect that he is going to leave you. To abandon you. And then you panic. There is something in your subconscious where you expect or want him to abandon you."

"I don't want him to abandon me. I don't understand."

"You'll just have to take the time to think about the dynamics of your relationships. There is something in this pattern where you expect or want the men to abandon you. Secondly, maybe you're choosing the wrong men. When you meet someone, before you get too far into the relationship, you should find out if you're both looking for the same thing. Tell them that you're looking for the house with the white picket fence and if they're not looking for the same thing, you have to move on. You have to change your behaviors; just a little twist and I think you will be able to achieve your goal. Now, does anyone else want to talk about their fears or phobias?"

Pavlovian response, sounds awful I thought as the woman next to me raised her hand to talk about her fear of flying. The rest of the class was interesting as people discussed everything from a fear of heights to a fear of changing jobs, but the instructor left me puzzled about my fear of abandonment. I had got a lot of figuring out to do.

The following night I met with Dr. Harill and I told him all about the class I had taken and when I asked him what he thought about the Pavlovian dog and bell theories, and how they related to human relationships.

"Well, I'm not sure what I think about that theory. He sounds like a behaviorist; I'm a cognitive therapist. I believe your problems stem from low self-esteem and we have to work on that."

"I don't always feel insecure. Sometimes I do, depending on the situation, but the majority of the time I don't feel like I have low self-esteem."

"That's because it's *unconscious*. It comes out in your behaviors and whom you choose to associate with. You may not feel like you have low self-esteem but you don't act as though you like yourself."

"Unconscious Low Self Esteem? That's horrible! Wait a minute, I just realized something. Many times when I get upset with myself besides saying idiot that I am, I also call myself a *jerk*. When I gave Robert the care package. I said to

him 'You're going to think I'm a big *jerk*.' Whenever my father was mad at me he would always say, 'Don't be a silly
jerk.' Is this is the perception I got of myself?"

"Parents have to be very careful what they say to their
children. The mistakes they make can be damaging to a
child's self esteem."

"But if these reactions and perceptions are totally *unconscious*, how am I ever going to do anything about it if I'm
not aware of it?"

"You have to be more conscious of this self-deprecating
language and begin saying 'no' to the unacceptable behaviors of others."

"You mean like the behaviors of Robert?"

"Yes."

"He's such a liar."

"Then why do you accept the behavior, Marianne?"

Feeling a little surprised at the question, I said, "I don't
know. Maybe because my father used to tell me it was okay
to tell white lies. He used to categorize his lies. Big lies were
a sin, white lies were okay. And I think in certain areas,
Robert has a neurosis similar to my father's. Not that my
father would ever operate like Robert. My father never
cheated on my mother, and my father is really a very nice
man, and I love him very much, but he is neurotic and has
a tremendous amount of anxiety, as does Robert Brenner.
For instance, whenever I want to confront my father about
something he may have done wrong or an emotionally
charged issue, he either denies it or he changes the subject.
Robert does the same thing. Why do people change the subject when confronted about something?

"There's a story about a diver who's in the water and he
sees a shark coming. So, in order not to get attacked by the

shark he does everything he can to distract the shark."

"Oh, I get it. Sometimes I feel like my father and mother's scene was Jaws I and my scene with Robert is Jaws II. There is definitely something about Robert that reminds me of my father. I guess that's why I was attracted to him."

"With romantic chemistry our reactions can also be *unconscious.* We are attracted to members of the opposite sex who exhibit the positive as well as the negative traits that exist in our parents."

"The negative traits? Why?"

"Because the negative traits carry the most weight in our attraction. Because incidents of neglect, abuse, criticism, or indifference affect our survival, they are more deeply etched in the unconscious than the memories of caring and attention. They are aching wounds that need to be healed. This is frustrating, because *consciously* we seek only the positive traits in a potential partner, so that we can get our needs met. But without the negative we wouldn't be attracted in the first place."

"So, what you're telling me is our mate selection is unconscious?"

"Yes. You see, the brain is like a computer. Everything that happened to you in childhood is stored in your memory and has trickled down into the unconscious. All our experiences in life are taken in as bytes of information. Imprinted in our minds. And when we meet someone who exhibit traits similar to our parents, our brain it makes a connection, a match and you are attracted to that person. But, it doesn't have to be that way, Marianne. We don't have to marry people like our parents."

"I recently read that children from dysfunctional homes

often have a *high tolerance* for inappropriate behavior. Our parents' behavior is our model. We have no reference point for what is normal, healthy or appropriate."

"Unfortunately, that's true. But you are a survivor, Marianne. As you recover and heal you will begin to recognize inappropriate behavior and you will not accept it. You will be able to create boundaries for yourself. You'll see, over time some nice change will occur. But change occurs slowly. The first step is recognition."

"But if I'm attracted to the wrong type of men, how do I stop the cycle?"

"Try going out with different types of people. Maybe someone you're not instantly attracted to. Let the chemistry develop. Take things more slowly. What's the rush?"

I felt the session with Dr. Harill went well, but the idea of unconscious low self-esteem and romantic chemistry was really upsetting to me. Scary stuff. That, along with the Pavlovian way of responding to men, was enough to send me over the edge.

My depression over Robert continued over the next few days so I set up an appointment with Reverend Allison. He always seems to help me put things in perspective. I have to stop thinking about Robert. I have to hang it up. Put it to bed. It was always good to see Reverend Allison and when I knocked on his office door and was greeted so warmly I instantly felt better.

"Hi, Marianne! Good to see you. You look terrific!"

"Well, I don't feel so terrific," I said while taking the cappuccino's I had brought out of the bag and handing him one. "It's over between Robert and me. He's not leaving the woman he lives with. Why am I having such a hard time forgetting him?"

"Because you have a tendency to fantasize. You not only had yourself married but you already had plans to give away the money!"

I laughed and said, "Well, I was going to give this church a lot of money."

"Aw, shucks!" the Rev said snapping his fingers and shaking his head.

"I wonder if I fantasized as a kid."

"Of course you did, that's how you survived."

"You're right. I used to fantasize about living in a family like *Leave It To Beaver*. It's funny because I even put a personal ad in a few years ago with a headline: *June Cleaver looking for Ward*." We both got a laugh out of that one.

Feeling sad again I asked, "But why did God bring Robert to me? I know why--He wanted to blow up larger than life what I've been doing for the past twenty five years."

"I believe we have choices. Why did you *choose* Robert?"

"I don't know. But what about all the coincidences?" I asked with my heart sinking, feeling awfully sad.

"Maybe they weren't all coincidences. Maybe not all of them had a message, but some did."

"But, I still care about him."

"It is taking you a long time to give up on Robert. How many times did you see him?"

"About eight times. "

"Why did he have such a profound effect on you?"

"I don't know. Because of this crazy chemistry. We were like magnets."

"It takes a lot more than chemistry. What did Robert give you? He deceived you, he strung you along."

"He only behaves the way he does because of his problems."

"Yes, but he has to be responsible for his actions! Prisoners have problems too, but do you think we should just let them commit crimes and not punish them?"

"You don't think he cared about me?" I asked tears streaming down my cheeks.

"I can see it's important for you to believe he cared about you, but I think you were his fantasy. His fantasy was fulfilled but was yours?"

"No," I answered and sat back in my chair. I then asked, "Do you think he loves the woman he's living with?"

"Of course not. How can he operate the way he does and at the same time love her. I believe he's a coward. He had an opportunity with you but he didn't take it. It's time to move on, Marianne.

"You're right. I've got to put him out of my mind."

I left Reverend Allison's office feeling totally miserable.

SPECIAL BIRTHDAY HOROSCOPE

When I woke up on the morning of my forty-first birthday, I began contemplating on all I had learned during the past year. No, things didn't work out with Robert and me. He was a lesson in life. If I hadn't met Robert, I probably wouldn't have gone into therapy, so some good has come out of this whole ordeal. I've also learned a tremendous amount about myself. I've been able to remove myself from myself and look down upon the scenes in my life, and I certainly have begun to understand where my insecurities stem from with the release of some very profound blocked memories. It has been a very painful journey so far, but that is all part of the process.

In the words of Rollo May from his book *Freedom and Destiny*, despair may lead to the deepest insight and most valuable change. Despair should be experienced constructively, as an opportunity. The despair can then act upon the person like the flood in Genesis: It can clear away the vast debris--the false answers, superficial principles---and leave the way open for new possibilities. That is for new freedom. In psychotherapy, times of despair are essential to one's discovery of hidden capacities and basic assets. If one never feels despair, it is doubtful whether he or she will feel anything below the surface.

The purpose of psychotherapy is for people to gain freedom. Free, as far as possible, from symptoms, whether they be psychosomatic symptoms like ulcers or psychological symptoms like acute shyness. Free from compulsions perpetually to choose partners of the opposite sex who cause continual unhappiness and continual punishment. That is the area in which I seek my freedom.

Why did I put up with all of Robert Brenner's bullshit? All the signs were there. Why didn't I pick up the phone at the beginning of the relationship and confront him as to why he wasn't available? A few weeks ago, and a few months too late, I did pick up the phone and I called him and asked him if he was happy with the woman he was living with. His answer was "Yes." Shocked, I asked him again. His answer again was "Yes." I then told him I had to give it up. I had to stop thinking about him. Dr. Harill told me that Freud once said falling in love is the closest thing to insanity. He was right.

The first coincidence with the newspaper article *The Late Blooming Groom* was a warning about his behavior. It was spelled out for me in black and white when it read, "*Men into a lot of casual sex sometimes don't want to get married because it restricts the opportunity for casual sex. Of course they won't admit it openly, but they feign love, feign commitment, exaggerate the depth of their feelings and basically tell women what they want to hear.*" Robert Brenner in a nutshell.

Now it was time for me to forget about Robert and get down to writing *my* book.

The next morning dragged but I got a chuckle reading my horoscope while riding to work. It read: Those who have discounted you will rue the day. Put aside insecurities and begin a new important project. Later that day, I had my usual session with Dr. Harill.

I read him the horoscope. He laughed and then asked, "But what did your *special* birthday horoscope say? You know, the one specifically for people born on November 30th."

"I don't know," I replied. The paper I read does not have a special birthday horoscope."

A few days later, I received a surprise in the mail, My Special Birthday Horoscope! My father had sent it to me without knowing anything about my meeting with Dr. Harill.

The horoscope read:

As someone once said, fate is an expensive schoolmaster but the fees are well worth paying if what you learn makes you happier, wiser, or more fulfilled. What takes place now is neither chance nor coincidence but a way of telling you to reach for goals you never knew existed.

I was shaking and started crying as I read the last part. I'm telling you, the horoscope itself was eerie, but the fact that Dr. Harill oddly questioned me about My Special Birthday Horoscope really made this another *Zapping* When I went back the following week and read him the horoscope, he had a freaked out look on his face. And when I showed the Horoscope to Reverend Allison, he also was shocked. "You know, you're pretty lucky; not too many people receive such strong messages," he said.

My life is one of animated suspense with all these coincidences, guiding me, leading me, and teaching me. To tell you the truth, it's kind of scary, never knowing when the next one will occur, but at the same time, it's exhilarating. Most times I feel so much more alive after one occurs, but sometimes they scare the shit out of me.

One thing I still don't understand is why I keep having these obsessive relationships. I feel embarrassed about Robert Brenner. Why would I even want to have anything to do with him? He's a creep. I should have dumped him a long time ago. But noooooooooo... I sent him letters, I pined over him, and I tried to rescue him wanting him to get into therapy. The whole thing was sickening. I could never have changed Robert. He's the only one who can do that. All the guys I've gone crazy over have been just like Robert. Emotionally unavailable and when they left, I sent them letters, I pined for them and then I schemed elaborate ways of getting them back. Crazy stuff. Sick neurotic behavior.

There was one guy Tim whom I dated for one month. On our first date, he told me to meet him at a bar downtown. When I got there he was talking to friends and ignored me the whole time. I told him how angry I was at his behavior and left. The next day Tim sent a small flowering begonia plant with a note attached: "Please forgive me." Tim was a funny guy, he was a lot of laughs so, foolishly I forgave him. The last time I saw him, we made love, he told me he loved me and I never heard from him again. Well, I devised an elaborate campaign to get Tim back. Why, I don't know. I sent him letters, I sent him flowers with a note attached—"Get Well Soon." I even played love songs on his message machine! All to no avail. Tim told me I should do this for someone who could appreciate it. It's sickening to think of what I went through to get this man to come back. It was so neurotic.

Then there was Dr. Gary, an Irish dentist, and someone I pined over for two years after we broke up. I really went crazy over this guy. After I met Dr. Gary, it took a week and a half for him to call. We went out, I fell "head over heels" as I usually do, but didn't see him for another two weeks. Dr. Gary told me he was very busy. In three months I saw Dr. Gary six times but I was madly in love with him. When I pressured him about us not seeing enough of each other, Dr. Gary stopped calling.

Did I accept the fact that he just wasn't available? NOOOOOOOO!! As usual, I sent him a letter, to which there was no response, and I pined over Dr. Gary for four months until finally, so desperate to see this wonderful man, I planned an elaborate party just so I could invite Dr. Gary. He accepted my invitation. It was a Lobster Luau to take place at my summer share home in the Hamptons on Memorial Day weekend. This was some party. I rented tables for the backyard. I had tropical floral arrangements with floating candles on all the tables. I had a huge exotic floral centerpiece and torches lining the perimeter of the tables. Something like the torch I was carrying around for this guy. All this to impress Dr. Gary and get him back into my arms.

Well, Dr. Gary did wind up back in my arms but, of course, this was only temporary. When I told him I wanted a relationship where I would see him once a week he balked although we planned on seeing each other again. We talked once after the party, but we had another blowout about his being unavailable and I never saw Dr. Gary after that. Did I get the message and finally give up on getting Dr. Gary back?   NOOOOOOOOOOOOOOOOOOOOOOOOOOOOOOO NOOOOOOOOOOOOOOOOO!! By the end of the summer I was planning another elaborate party, for Labor Day. A Yacht Party! I rented a 90-foot yacht and had everybody chip in forty dollars for liquor and food. Of course, Dr. Gary was invited free of charge. He told me he would think about the offer, but never called back. At this point, I knew it was time to move on. Unbelievable. I know I am a Wild and Crazy Girl but that was ridiculous! That is so embarrassing. How could I have act that way? This is called *obsessive* love. Why do I go through all this trouble for men who don't even care about me? Why? Why? Why?

SHAMPOO, CUT AND COINCIDENCE

I stepped off the elevator into the reception area of the hair salon hoping I would leave this place a happy woman. I needed a little boost to my self-esteem and usually my hairdresser, Jack, could accomplish that although some days he went a little too far, got a little too creative and I wound up leaving in a panic calculating how long it would take my hair to grow back to the length I came in with. But for the most part he had the magic touch and besides being my hairdresser he was also shrink number three. I was always asking his advice, talking incessantly about the men in my life. He was my confidant. He was my buddy.

I stepped up to the receptionist and told her I had a two o'clock with Jack. She told me there would be a little bit of a wait and offered me coffee or a soft drink as I took a seat in the waiting area. There was an array of magazines on the coffee table. As I scanned through them, I wondered if they contained any messages for me. Then I said to myself: You are being ridiculous! Here you go again looking for coincidences. I have to stop thinking like this. I'm getting carried away with this stuff.

The receptionist came by with my coffee. I thanked her as I picked up *Self* magazine and started scanning the magazine for any article of interest. There were articles on dieting, relationships, and sex. The three main ingredients in any woman's magazine today. I read through a few and picked up another magazine and looked through the table of contents. Nothing really interested me. You see, I said to myself, there are no messages here for you. It's all in your imagination. Just as I finished that thought, a woman seated way in the back of the salon, at least twenty feet away, said in a loud voice, "I DON'T DRINK BECAUSE MY MOTHER WAS AN ALCOHOLIC."

It was loud and clear, echoing through the whole place. I looked over and she was talking to Jack. Oh my God, I thought to myself. This is bizarre. I thought there were no messages here for me. I was shaking, nervous, my face was flushed as I shrunk back into my seat feeling the undertow of guilt grabbing at my heels. I began to think about my wild and crazy Friday nights. It's too much. It's one thing to go out and have a good time but this was continuous drinking throughout the evening. This wasn't one or two drinks. This was six, seven, up to eight drinks and sometimes even more than that. Hungover on Saturday. Thursday night's a big party night, too. Not to the same degree as Friday night. Maybe it's only three or four drinks on Thursday. Enough to give you a good buzz. All my friends were out doing the same thing. What does this mean? That we are all heavy drinkers. That's what it means.

"Jack's ready for you to get shampooed," the receptionist said. I rose slowly, still shaken and was trying to compose myself as I headed toward the shampoo station. As the warm water soaked my hair, I thought, my God, was this another coincidence? Is there a message here for me today? What road am I heading down?

I have to be careful, I thought. It's in my family. I am an adult child of an alcoholic. My mother's been dead for twelve years, but her ghost is very much alive. I feel stigmatized. "It's hereditary." "It runs in families." You hear it on news programs, you read it in articles.

A few weeks later I saw a program on television about alcohol abuse. They studied the drinking habits of college students. A good number of them turned out to be involved in binge drinking, which for a woman is drinking more than four drinks at one sitting; for men it is drinking more than five at one sitting. This is considered alcohol abuse.

Shortly thereafter, I read an article about a program for Alcohol Moderation. The limit for drinking in moderation is for women, a weekly intake of no more than nine drinks per week and for men the limit should be fourteen per week. I'd been tipping the scales on this one, drinking more like the male counterpart. I needed to make some changes.

The shampoo girl wrapped my hair in a towel and led me over to Jack's chair. He asked how I was and there were a few minutes of small talk, but for the most part, I was very quiet. I was really frightened by this experience. "Just a trim, Jack." I certainly didn't feel like experimenting with a new look. That would really send me over the edge. It was the inside of me that needed a new shape.

I immediately cut back my drinking to a more moderate level. These coincidences were hitting me like a Mack Truck, forcing me to take a look at my life. I was learning so much about myself and began sharing all this information with my friends. Oddly enough Winslow and I remained friends after we broke up. He was much kinder to me when we weren't dating.

Culture Clash they said. Our backgrounds couldn't have been any more different--on the surface that is. He was from old money. I was from no money. But on the inside our backgrounds were very similar. We both grew up in alcoholic homes. Winslow's mother and father were alcoholics. A Double Whammy. Both of them died young smoking and drinking themselves to death. Alcoholism and lung cancer. Winslow was following the same road. They removed a spot on his lung last year. But he continued to smoke incessantly, at least two packs a day.

He called me the other day. "Let's do a little boating today. Then we can go over to Indian Harbor Yacht Club for lunch." He was a generous soul but I could have killed him that day. The water was so rough. We shouldn't have gone out as far as we did. There were small craft warnings I didn't know about. The waves were so high that they hurled the bow of the boat ten feet in the air. Then the boat pounded down on the water so hard I could barely hold on, and at times I slammed into the side of the boat. Water from the waves sprayed into the boat, the wind swirled around us. Talk about a bad hair day. By the time we docked at Indian Harbor, I was a mess.

We sat down and had lunch and after the tables were cleared I began to tell Winslow about all the strange things that had been happening to me lately and about the blocked memories that came back to me. We both knew the pain of growing up enduring the cruelty of verbal abuse. It was a cutting pain that crushed our chances of developing a healthy self-esteem.

Winslow took a sip of his drink. He told me he was up to ten drinks a day. I began to tell him what I had learned. "All the problems in our adult lives stem from unresolved childhood conflicts that are directly linked to the traumatic events that occurred in our childhood. The hurt child inside. Your problems have to do with what happened to *little* Winslow. That's why you're smoking and drinking yourself to death today," I said tapping my hand on his heart.

I looked at Winslow and he started to cry. I turned to him and said, "I'm sorry Winslow, I didn't mean to hurt you."

He turned to me with his lips trembling saying, "I just saw a window of a scene from my childhood. 'You stupid, ugly child,' my mother said to me. I hated her. She was such a bitch. She was either ignoring me, slapping me for no reason or calling me stupid and ugly."

Winslow began sobbing intensely. My heart broke for him. "Let's get out of here," I said feeling awful.

"Give me a minute to compose myself," he said wiping his tears.

We got out to the parking lot where Winslow had left his car and I said to him, "You have to let it out, go back to your childhood, and grieve for what happened to you as a child. All the unresolved grief that's stuffed deep inside has been carried into your adulthood. When you go back and really look at what happened to you as a child, you'll find compassion for yourself Winslow. And through that compassion you'll develop self love."

"Will you be my anchor?" he asked as he held my hand.

"Of course I will, Winslow. You're a good friend and I'll help you in any way I can."

I arrived home from work a few weeks later and there was a message from Winslow. "Marianne, it's me, Winslow. There was an intervention in my home today. My family and friends came over and persuaded me to seek treatment. I'm taking an evening flight tonight and checking into Hazelton for four weeks. I'll be in touch. You take care now." I put my hands to my face and the tears began pouring out of me. I felt so bad for him but I was relieved he was getting help.

I was surprised to get a call from his son a few days later. I had only met him once. He was a tall, handsome young man of twenty-one years. "Marianne, this is John Barrett, Winslow's son. I would like to thank you because I think you had an influence on my father going into rehab."

"Why would you think that?" I asked.

"Well, I couldn't believe how easy it was to get him to go. And then he told me about the talk you two had a few weeks before. It must have had an affect on him because he was thinking about signing himself in. Basically, I think you had prepared him in some way because he was ready to go."

I was so surprised to get his message. Everything happened so quickly. I guess unknowingly our timing was perfect. Isn't it odd how we were both in sync?

STRUGGLING TO WRITE

Six months had passed since I set out to write, and I had written only twenty pages. What was holding me back? Take a wild guess. I N S E C U R I T Y. I must have written those twenty pages over twenty times, always second-guessing myself and over analyzing. I was finally happy with what I had written so far, but it had been a real struggle, a never-ending battle with the ego. At the rate I was going, the book would be finished by the end of the next millennium. Too many excuses, too many nights staring at the blank screen and giving up too easily. A never ending see-saw of building up my ego, urging myself to go on, to try, but then only to knock it down again, eventually losing the battle to the greater side of the ego, the one that time and time again pulverizes me into feeling I'm not good enough.

I packed up the word processor and headed off to Newport, Rhode Island. I'd taken a share in a summer- house for the month of August with Patti and a group of friends, mostly from Brett's. This would be my first time up to the house and I was also on vacation that week, so when the weekenders in the house cleared out on Sunday, I would be going in for the final round with the ego. I had to finish writing this book. God, it might be my ticket out of the Garment Center.

It was a bright sunny day and the view of Newport was breathtaking as I drove my car over the bridge. Founded in 1639, Newport is a beautiful town that became a popular summer retreat for the wealthy back in the late 1800's. The Vanderbilts, the Astors and the like all built opulent mansions concentrated along Newport's Bellevue Avenue that they called "summer cottages." The Newport Preservation Society now maintains seven of these mansions and they are open to the public. The wealth was unbelievable, so excessive that one wanders through these icons in a constant state of amazement. The most one can digest is three Mansions a day or else you will O.D. on these opulent, grandiose, gilded structures developing what I call the Mansion Glaze exiting these palaces with eyes glazed and tongue hanging out.

I opened my pocketbook fumbling for the directions to the house. The car bumped up and down on the cobblestone streets as I strained my eyes looking for Tenth Street. It was late afternoon as the glaring sun setting in the distance was blinding me. Almost missing it, I made a quick right just in time to scan the street for number 132. The house was on the left and I immediately fell in love with it. It was a huge, three story, yellow saltbox probably built in the late 1800's. The green shutters, flower boxes filled with red geraniums and the American flag waving from the second story completed the vision. I was happy. It was a beautiful house from the outside and I hoped the inside would be just as much a delight.

I pulled into the small narrow driveway, grabbed a few bags of luggage and made my ascent up the three steps leading to the front door. I looked under the doormat, found the key and opened the door to a very charming living room, decorated with a very interesting eclectic summer cottage mix. A tad under the price range of the Vanderbilts "summer cottage" look, but very cozy. The wood floors made from wide planks of pine had to be the original and the antique farmhouse dining room table and beautiful fireplace in the living room made this a perfect setting for writing. No excuses now, although I'm sure I'd try to find one.

The house was empty. There was a note on the kitchen table from Patti, Christine and Peter saying they had gone to the store to pick up some groceries for dinner. I lugged my suitcases up three flights of stairs and when I finally reached my room, I piled the suitcases in the corner of the room and collapsed on the bed. It was a pretty room with an antique bed, a white chenille bedspread, an old chest, and a beautifully framed print that hung above the bed. The print was of a woman lying down, eyes closed with an angel kissing her while she slept. I loved it. I rested for a while but soon heard the rumblings of the other house members, so I got up to greet my friends.

They were in the kitchen unpacking the groceries for dinner. They bought so much food—steak, pasta, corn, salad and wine.

There goes my diet.

I chipped in ten dollars to cover my share and we all began to prepare for tonight's grand barbecue. It was a wonderful group effort and everything went smoothly. Before you knew it we were stuffing our faces and toasting the new summerhouse. During dinner we decided to go to the Candy Store, a club down by the harbor in the center of town. Everything was within walking distance of the house, which was good for those who might be stumbling home tonight.

Everybody helped clean up after dinner and then we headed upstairs to get ready for our night on the town.

Newport is centered on the harbor. As we strolled towards town, the lights from the restaurants, clubs and boutiques blending in with the sails from the huge boats docked harbor-side made a beautiful backdrop for this very picturesque part of town. The noise, the traffic, and the tourist population increased as we grew closer and closer to the Harbor's center.

We popped in and out of boutiques, finally ending up at the Candy Store where the line to get in was five deep. I'd been to Newport three times and still hadn't made it into this club. It was always too crowded. We decided to forego the lines and head for Newport Blues, a new blues and jazz club across the street from the harbor.

The club was very attractive, large open area, with huge twenty-foot ceilings and walls lined with tall, very imposing windows encased in thick panels of polished oak. It used to be an old bank. The centerpiece was a tremendous vault that remains in its original spot. Very cleverly designed. We had a great time, dancing, partying, and laughing closing the place at twelve-thirty.

Sunday morning, I was up early and decided to go to the pretty stone church around the corner. The pews were half empty. What has happened to spirituality in this country? It's sad really. I hope there are churches left on this planet a hundred years from now. At this rate they might turn into museums. But, look at me, I only recently got in touch with my spirituality. A year ago I was like a lot of people. I believed in God, went to church on Easter and Christmas and I rarely prayed. My shrink, Dr. Harill told me that there are four sides to man: The emotional, physical, intellectual and spiritual. In order to be a whole person, all four must be in working order. I was lacking in the emotional area, not understanding what was wrong, but by getting in touch with the spiritual side of my life I was beginning to change and I thank God everyday for all he has given me.

On the walk back to the house, I stopped at the corner deli to pick up some donuts and bagels for the house. When I returned, part of the crew was still in bed. Carol was at the coffee machine with tousled hair and blood-shot eyes. I was glad I didn't drink as much as my housemates who partied after we got back from Newport Blues. It was really like an animal house last night. Everyone was bombed; my old boyfriend was hitting on me, this one trying to pick that one up and eventually some of these inebriated love birds wound up in the sack with each other. There was something dreadfully wrong with the picture. So, when the after-hour partying began, I had a bowl of cereal and went to bed--ALONE! I'm just not into this heavy partying anymore.

The next afternoon turned out to be a pleasant one. We drove along Ocean Drive and stopped at Hammersmith Farm, which once was the Kennedy's summer home. The estate was breathtaking and as I looked out upon the emerald green grounds that stretched to the water's edge and then over to the magnificent gardens. I was lost in the splendor of this beauty.

My mind wandered to imagine the wedding reception of John Kennedy and Jacqueline Bouvier, because this is where it took place. I was reminded of the Days of Camelot. Why was this a time so fondly remembered? Was it just the glamour of the Kennedy family or was it also the sense of community, the strong values and respect for fellow man that made this time the Days of Camelot? Then my mood changed as I thought of the assassination. The death of JFK was, to me, the forefront to the decaying of society. The country went to pot after that, literally. That's when the drug culture emerged, the sexual revolution occurred, the divorce rate soared and we topped it off with a loss of spirituality.

The country went into a tailspin of moral decline. Many people think the war was responsible for the fallen society. But can everything be blamed on the Vietnam War? How about the loss of spirituality? Perhaps that was the forefront to the sorry state of this country. My spirit was sinking when I left this beautiful estate.

It was late afternoon when we drove over to the Inn at Castle Hill, a popular place set upon a hill that overlooks the ocean. We pulled into the parking lot and began the hike up the hill that led us to the social event of the day, Sunday afternoon on the green. The place was packed as we made our way to the outdoor bar to order drinks. We spread out a quilt, sat cross-legged to shoot the breeze as we checked out the single guys walking by while sipping Sea Breeze's. The sun began to set over the ocean. The view was spectacular.

The evening came and when we got back to the house everyone started to pack up for the trip home. Except for me, of course. I'll be here all week with my word processor.

To tell the truth, I'm looking forward to having the place to myself. After the last person left, I just took it easy for the rest of the evening reading, and watching a little television. Tomorrow will be a big writing day. I'll get up early, take a little jog, have a little breakfast and start writing by nine a.m. Then I'll take an hour for lunch and write until five. I'm going to put in a full day.

I climbed into bed around eleven and became a little nervous as I thought about writing my book. I was insecure and hoped I could accomplish what I had set out to do. I decided to pray really hard. I prayed and prayed and prayed saying a full rosary. I know it might sound corny, but that's how this whole deal started so I stuck with it. The rosary worked for me. It doesn't matter how one prays, the important thing is to pray, and that I did...God, please give me the confidence to write this book. I'm nervous. I'm scared. I need your help. Please God, please give me the confidence to write this book. After a good half hour of prayer and asking God to give me confidence to write, I tried to get some sleep. I was tossing and turning unable to fall asleep. A few minutes later I got up to go to the bathroom.

When I sat down on the pot, I noticed a *Reader's Digest* sitting on the sink vanity. I picked it up and brought it back into the bedroom. I got back into bed, pulled the covers up over me and since I couldn't sleep I began to read through the magazine. I came to the section called Personal Glimpses that was highlighting the lives of three stars, one of them being the famous writer, Michael Crichton. He wrote *Jurassic Park*, *Disclosure*, *Rising Sun* and many other well-known books.

Best-selling novelist, Michael Crichton always wanted to be a writer. But as an undergraduate at Harvard he found *the standards of the English department impossibly high. Frustrated, he submitted an essay written by George Orwell for an assignment on <u>Gulliver's Travels</u>. When the paper got a B-Minus, Crichton decided to become a doctor instead. "I had read somewhere that there are only about 200 Americans who can make a living from writing full time," He said, "I thought, I can't be one of 200 people in America. That's too hard."*

*To pay bills while attending Harvard Medical School, however, Crichton wrote thrillers. Then he published The Andromeda Strain, an immediate hit. He never bothered with his medical internship...*MY HEART IS POUNDING AND I CAN NOT BELIEVE THIS! GULLIVER'S TRAVELS? Two minutes ago I had prayed very heavily for God to give me the confidence to write my book. I picked up an old *Reader's Digest* from November 1994, which happened to be the month I started writing this book, and inside was an article about a despondent Michael Crichton, thinking he could never become a professional writer, but going on to write a bestseller that was made into a movie! And he cheated on an assignment about GULLIVER'S TRAVELS! What were the chances of this happening? Was this just a coincidence? OH MY GOD! WHAT'S HAPPENING HERE? GULLIVER'S TRAVELS MUST BE SOME KIND OF CODE WORD!

I finished fifty pages by the end of the week. Six months later, I had half the book completed with a total of one hundred twenty-five pages written! Nothing like a little push from up above to get you going.

ANSWERED PRAYERS

The rain was pelting down upon the hood of my car as I wiped the thick fog from the inside of my windshield and turned right onto Field Point Road. Memories came to mind as I passed by the old Victorian house that was once known as Brett's. They closed Brett's about a month ago. The end of an era. To me in some strange way, it symbolizes a closing of the old book of my life and a beginning anew.

I'm not into heavy drinking anymore. I don't feel the need, and I don't like it anymore. I still go out, and once in and a while I do slip and drink too much. But for the most part everything has been tempered to a moderate level. Since I have gotten to know myself, my anxiety level has decreased tremendously and I am much happier than I was before.

In his book, *Man's Search for Himself*, Rollo May makes an analogy of self-awareness to that of driving a car. The less aware you are of how to drive a car, or of the traffic conditions you are driving through, the more tense you are and the firmer hold you have to keep on yourself. But on the other hand, the more experienced you are as a driver and the more conscious you are of the traffic problems and what to do in emergencies, the more you can relax at the wheel with a sense of power. You have the awareness that it is you who is doing the driving and you are in control.

Consciousness of self actually expands our control of our lives, and with that expanded power comes the capacity to let ourselves go. The more consciousness of one's self one has, the more spontaneous and creative one can be at the same time. To undertake this "venture of becoming aware of ourselves" is to discover the sources of inner strength and security, which are the rewards for such a venture.

I pulled into the church parking lot; I was excited about the news I had for the Rev. I sat down on his soft, cushiony couch I've become accustomed to over the last year and looked across at the warm, kind, funny, and wonderful man who has stood by my side through this whole experience. I feel nothing but complete gratitude for all he has given me.

"Well, I think I figured it out."

"What's that, Marianne?"

"The other day, I was reviewing all I have learned this year. I've learned that our problems are caused by unre-solved childhood conflicts directly related to traumatic events of the past. *Unconsciously*, these unresolved conflicts are carried into adulthood and are directly related to our insecurities, sensitivities, over-reactions, neurotic and self-destructive behaviors.

I then began to link the traumatic events in my past to some of my behaviors and discovered why my love relation-ships have been *obsessive love*.

First of all, I have a fear of abandonment which, I believe, was caused by my father going away on business five
days a week, for four to six months a year from the time I
was seven until I was twelve. It was especially traumatic for
me because the first time he had to travel for business may
have been around the same time I had that incident with
my mother telling me to go to hell and with my father subsequently explaining to me that my mother had a disease;
that she was an alcoholic. So, all these things happened
and then my father left. He took off. He abandoned me. How
could he have done that?" I asked tears welling up in my
eyes.

"He was probably scared, so he minimized your mother's
alcoholism."

"I'm not going to blame my father and mother for the
mistakes they made. My mother was sick and I know my
father never meant to hurt me. He was hurting and con-
fused himself. I love my father and I only wish I could have
better loved my mother. She had a very kind, compassion-
ate core but it was drowned out in alcohol. I only wish she
could have solved her problems. I wonder what her family
dynamics were. I knew she hated her mother, she was in
denial about her father's alcoholism, and she was a daddy's
girl, just like me. She must have been in a tremendous
amount of psychological pain to drink the way she did. It's
just a shame. She probably didn't get the love she deserved
either.

And my father wanted to see my mother as the woman
he married, so he minimized her alcoholism. All this denial,
and repression are passed down from generation to generation, but the buck stops here.

My parents' generation was ignorant of the psychological care a child needs. It's really nobody's fault, they just didn't know how. They thought food, clothing and shelter did the trick. People aren't taught how to be parents. It's the toughest job in the world without any training."

"You're a very perceptive young lady, Marianne. You're right, it's nobody's fault. They just didn't know how."

"Anyway, getting back to my discoveries, a few months ago, I took a course on overcoming fears and phobias. I told the teacher I had a fear of abandonment and I was attracted to men who were emotionally unavailable and who had a fear of commitment. He told me that my reactions to men were unconscious, that they were Pavlonian in nature and that in some way I expect or want men to abandon me.

I didn't believe I wanted men to abandon me, but I felt, there was something to what he was saying. I have a tendency to idealize men, because my father, regardless of the mistakes he made in parenting, was the parent from whom I received love. Looking back on my dating life, the men who had the most effect on me were the ones who weren't available. As soon as a guy showed signs of taking off or of "abandoning" me, this is when I went...N U T S!! These are the men who turned me on! Their taking off triggered an irrational emotional response. *Unconsciously* I would relate it to the unresolved conflict of my father abandoning me. When a man left, even if it was only after a month of dating, I over-reacted. I took it much harder than I should have.

I would send the letters, the gifts and I would pine over these guys for months, even years just like I pined over my father when he left. These are the men I idealized. Instead of saying to myself, this guy's just not interested move on, I put them on a pedestal going to all kinds of extremes to get them to come back: unconscious, irrational behavior all related to continuously trying to resolve the childhood conflict of my fathers abandoning me. That's got to be it."

"I absolutely agree. You figured it out, Marianne. Ultimately what did these men do? They all abandoned you."

"God, I remember the scene with Robert Brenner in the parking lot of Brett's. I was confronting him, wanting to know what was going on as to why he was never available. He was a nervous wreck and wanted to bolt out of that parking lot. He started up his car and began pulling out saying, 'I'll call you tomorrow, I've got to go, I've got to go.' And I'm holding onto his car's door handle, knees bent, screaming, 'NO, DON'T GO! NO, DON'T GO!'

"That was a scene directly out of my childhood. My father pulling out of the driveway, going away on business, with me holding on to his door handle for dear life, tears streaming down my face, hysterically crying, "DADDY, PLEASE DON'T GO! DADDY, PLEASE DON'T GO!"

"I think your theory is correct. You've hit the nail on the head."

"This has really been an unbelievable journey. A purging of the soul. Very painful at times, but experiencing the pain is a vital ingredient for ultimately experiencing joy. One has to put together the puzzle of life in order to have a sense of self."

"Understanding what makes you tick, leads to com- passion for yourself which ultimately unfolds the love you need most of all: self love. I can't tell you how much you've grown over the past year. I wish I had a video of you when you first walked into this office. There's a real metamorphosis happening here. A self-actualization. You have a lot to celebrate, Marianne."

"You're right, and besides all the nice changes that have

occurred within myself, what about this book? I've discovered a hidden talent. I've actually written a book! That in itself is a miracle. I had the confidence to write a book and I am so very proud of what I've accomplished. I am so thankful for all of God's help."

"I think you might be changing careers soon, Marianne."

"Wouldn't that be wonderful? The gift of writing this book was an extra bonus. I only prayed for two things. For God to bring me a husband, and for him to help me solve my problems. No, He didn't plop a husband down from the heavens. I guess He really can't do that because we have choices in life. But He gave me something far greater. He gave me the gift of my True Self. He gave me the tools that will enable me to have a healthy relationship.

"Now that I've figured this out, I can't imagine reacting the way I used to when a guy broke up with me. My letter writing days are over. Even though they were pretty funny-- in a sick way.

"And I definitely don't take men home from bars anymore. Don't even kiss them on a first date.

"But the greatest gift of all is the self-love I've developed. My best friend is me! To love and cherish forever. And I've learned it's okay to be single. Of course I would love to find my life's partner but if I don't, I'll be okay. I've got plenty of friends in the same boat as I am. It seems to be an epidemic today. Successful, attractive, self-reliant single women in their forties. But relationships are important and there have been two men in my life since Robert and neither one has strung me along, both being very responsible in keeping in touch with me, calling regularly. But, the latest one, Keith, started putting me down after a couple of months. I don't want this guy or anything that resembles him."

"You only spent a couple of months with this man, and you recognized what was happening. You're getting much better at this game. You're not sitting home crying. You're not pining over him. That's the beauty of this experience. When he mistreated you, you were able to kiss him good-bye and move on to the next,"

"That's true. If I were able to do that in my twenties, I would have been married. I am sorry I waited so long to get the help I sorely needed. I'm fortunate though because some people never solve their problems. But, I am getting better and better. More and more in control of my life. The driving is getting easier and easier and pretty soon I'll be on----CRUISE CONTROL!"

Now here's another coincidence for you non-believers. This one is up there on the Richter Scale of Coincidences. The other day I walked into the office and said good morning to Joe, my boss. His grouchy reply was, "Get all those patterns out we fit yesterday!" What's wrong with him, I thought. An hour or so later he came into my office with the J.C. Penney's report on three garments I submitted for fit approval.

"Approved, Approved, Not Approved. Why weren't all these garments approved the first time?"

"Joe, you know J.C. Penney's is tough and it's not uncommon for them to ask for a corrected garment to be submitted. I don't understand why you're acting this way. Is something wrong?"

"Why do you ask that?"

"Because you're not treating me right." Then he left the papers on my table and started to walk away. He then turned around and in front of all my co-workers said,

"You're lucky I'm such a nice guy or I would have fired you a long time ago!"

Outraged, my adrenalin began to surge, face turning red, heart pounding I turned to him and said, "No, you're lucky I'm such a good patternmaker!!"

He replied smugly, "All my patternmakers are good!" and walked out of the room. I was burning, livid. I called my message machine at home with a reminder to call all my previous fit models to see if there were any jobs available in the market.

I ran into Kathy's office in a rage, telling her what happened. Debbie, Joe's sister who is also Kathy's assistant, was in the room and tried to calm me down saying Joe didn't mean what he said. "Don't listen to him, he's just in a bad mood," she told me. I didn't care. I was leaving.

I went back into my room still so upset that I decided to say a prayer...*Our Father, who art in heaven, hallowed be thy name, thy kingdom come, thy will be done on earth as it is in heaven. Give us this day our daily bread and forgive us for our trespasses as we forgive those who trespass against us and lead us not into temptation but deliver us from evil. Amen.*

God, it's time for me to go. I've got to leave this place. I'd like to leave the whole industry and maybe someday I will find a way out, but for now I have to look for another job. If ever I leave this industry I'd like to go out with dignity. This is a dead end job with terrible working conditions and minimal raises and bonuses. Now, Joe treats me like this. I have to find a new job, but I need the confidence to go out there again. I've had so many bad experiences in this industry, but I have to get past those and move on. God, please, please, give me the confidence to move on, to find a new job.

Half an hour later, out of the clear blue, a head hunter made a *cold* call to my company, asked the receptionist to speak to a patternmaker. She just happened to transfer the call to me. I picked up the phone to hear, "Hello this is Danny Santoro from Pacesetters Employment Agency. I'm looking for a Missy Dress Production Patternmaker. *Do you know anyone who is looking for a job?*"

I started to shake and almost fell off my chair as I answered, "Why yes, I happen to be looking for a job."

"Great, the position that's available is for a Better Dress house. Fax me your resume and I'll get back to you."

"Fine, I'll fax it out tomorrow and we'll talk after you receive it."

"Sounds good to me. Talk to you tomorrow." I hung up the phone, and saw Ida, my fellow patternmaker, walking out of the room. She was a witness to the whole fiasco this morning. "Ida, I have to talk to you," I frantically yelled out to her.

"Marianne, what's the matter?" she said.

"YOU'RE NEVER GOING TO BELIEVE WHAT JUST HAPPENED!"

"What is it??"

"A head hunter just called to ask if I knew of anyone looking for a job as a Missy Dress Production Patternmaker! God's blowing me out of my chair!"

"Oh my God. I can't believe it. You've been *Zapped* again! That's so strange." We both just looked at each other shaking our heads with frightful looks on our faces.

The next morning, I faxed my resume on my way to the office. Meanwhile, I had to clear the air with my boss for the remaining time I would be working for him. I walked into his office first thing in the morning and said, "Good morning, Joe. Yesterday afternoon was very upsetting to me and I would like to clear the air, but first I have to know what I did wrong."

"Wrong? You did nothing wrong. Upset? I'm not upset." he calmly replied.

"Excuse me Joe, but yesterday afternoon you told me "I was lucky you were such a nice guy or you would have fired me along time ago."

"Well, actually at that time, I was thinking about when you came in late after the snow storm and screamed at me."

He'd been repressing the issue he had with me.

"You're right, Joe, I shouldn't have yelled at you. I should have talked to you because I was also upset. That incident happened two days after the Blizzard of '96. It had been announced over the radio and television that the trains were not running on schedule. It took me three hours to get home the night before. I was fifteen minutes late the following morning and when I passed your office, you called me back, gave me a look, and started tapping on your watch. That was upsetting to me. I was also upset with the fact that your brother, David, gave me a hard time when I called in *during the blizzard* and told him I wouldn't be able to make it in. There was a state of emergency in effect."

"Listen, we are all just here to make a living. You don't realize how expensive it is to run this place. It costs ten thousand dollars just to turn the lights on in the morning. We need our employees to be on time and please try to cut down on the personal phone calls. You're only allowed three personal phone calls per day or else I'm going to tell the receptionist to take a message." He then walked over to me put his arm around me and said, "Okay, I've forgiven you, we're friends again, now go back to work." I smiled, looked up at Joe and said, "Alright." and walked out of the room thinking he is out of his mind to believe that our relationship has been normalized after that speech. He's forgiven me. Big Deal!

The new company is Samantha Lee, a better dress firm and I am really excited about this opportunity. The company carries a line I could be proud of. I might be able to kiss J.C. Penney's good-bye. I walked into my interview very impressed with the working conditions as they had a beautiful plant in the fitting room, everything was clean and organized and each patternmaker had a personal file cabinet for records. Where I currently work, I have a dilapidated plastic stacker on my table and there are tiles missing from the ceiling above my head.

The Production Manager, Mr. Jerry Mancini, warmly greeted me, we sat down to review my industry experience with him and afterwards he turned to me to say, "This is like no other company in the Garment Center. It is a peaceful, quiet atmosphere; there is no yelling and screaming. We offer a 401k plan with matching funds, profit sharing, medical and dental benefits. You are reviewed after three months and we talk to you about areas you may or may not need to work on. Every year you are reviewed for a raise. You don't have to start fuming about the raise you didn't get, feeling totally unappreciated, like you usually have to do in this business. You automatically get an annual raise and bonus."

"Wow! Sounds like a great place to work."

"It really is very different. It's a very nice place to work. Your background looks good. We'll communicate through the headhunter as to your salary requirements and we'll talk soon. It was pleasure meeting you." We stood up, shook hands, and he walked me to the door.

I was on cloud nine when I left the place. This is a dream job, like no other place in the Garment Center! It could have been just another crappy company in the industry, but this one has benefits up the Wazoo! Oh God, I hope I get this job. A few hours after my interview, I called my headhunter for the inside scoop. "Hello Danny, it's Marianne. I was wondering if you heard anything from Jerry Mancini?"

"As a matter of fact, I just got off the phone with him. He said you did great. He felt you could definitely handle the job, it's only a matter of salary."

A few days ago I got a call from Danny. Jerry Mancini wanted to see me for a second interview. I'm on my way over there as we speak. I'm confident, I'm looking good and I've got the feeling everything is going my way. Wish me luck!

THE GREATEST COINCIDENCE OF ALL

A few months after I started my *new* job, I met an Englishman who revealed to me the greatest coincidence of all. He came from an aristocratic background. His grandfather was a Knight, Sir Arthur F. Smith. Before he went off to fight in WW1 his father gave him a small bible. On the flyleaf he wrote: "Because thou hast made the Lord thy refuge... there shall no evil befall the...For He shall give His angels charge over thee, to keep thee in all thy ways."(Psalm 91: 9-11.)

Smith put the bible in his hip pocket and went off to war. Soon after, he was shot in the butt and thrown to the other side of the road. Shaken but not badly injured, he removed the pocket bible to discover the bullet entered the bible but had stopped midway and landed directly on Psalm 91. The bullet then turned sideways and exited between the very pages of this Psalm. This is a documented story and of course, was more than just coincidence. It was a miracle.

THE TEAM OF ANGELS

So, that's the story of *Zapped.* I've spent four years trying to get this book published. It was my trip to Peru that
finally set the works in motion and my angels helped me
every step of the way in getting this book published. When I
went to find a book cover designer they were at it again. I
called ten graphic designers I picked out from the Yellow
Pages.

The only one that specialized in book covers was a company called Design Advantage. I made an evening appointment with the owner of the firm, to look at the covers she
has designed.

I arrived at the downtown office, and was very impressed with her work. I told her what the book was about
and she seemed very interested. When we finished she
asked if she could walk me to the train. I said I wasn't going
straight home, that I was going to stop and have dinner at
the Mexican restaurant down the street. "I think I'll join

you," she said.

This is a pushy broad, I thought.

But then she said, "Well, I want to find out more about the book. I'm from a very dysfunctional family too."

"Well my mother was an alcoholic," I said.

"Mine was too," she replied. I felt an instant connection to her. Kindred spirits.

We wound up having a wonderful dinner together and I told her the whole story. During our conversation I discovered that she grew up in *Levittown*, the same town I did, and she was a *former book editor*. She asked me to send her the manuscript. She read it and edited it at no charge! That was a wonderful gift.

I've had four editors in total. All kind and generous people. Mary Lee was my first. My angels were up to their tricks again with this one. She was a member of my church. One evening I had gone down to the church to have my picture taken for the church pictorial. I filled out a card with my name, address, and telephone number and handed it to the woman in charge. "Oh my God, I can't believe it!" she screeched. "I used to live in the exact same apartment as you!" Mary Lee was the tenant right before me. I moved into my apartment after she moved out, but our first meeting was at the church that night. We became friends and she was my first editor.

Then came Peggy. She is a member of my church and was a former journalist at *Time* magazine. She donated a year of her time with the first major editing of my book. What a tremendous help she has been to me.

Writing a book is very difficult. I had to devote every weekend and all my vacation time for a year and a half to complete this book. One's insecurities always pop up. I'm very sensitive about my book. I can take criticism from people I know are truly supportive but oddly enough, it's your family and close friends that will be least supportive. One particular friend, I won't name names but she knows who she is, said one evening, "I don't know about the title. What's *Zapped*? I don't get it?" That along with her total disinterest in the book sent me over the edge.

I was so upset, I decided to take a survey to find out how the general public would respond to the title *Zapped*. But I would also give them some additional choices. I printed out the back cover text and listed three possible titles at the bottom of the page. I would take it on the train the next day and ask women sitting next to me if they would like to participate in title selection.

The first woman I asked seemed very conservative and I didn't know if she was the type of woman would buy my book but I asked her any way. She picked the title *The Power of Synchronicity*. Just as suspected...Bad taste.

My next stop was going to be lunch at Starbuck's on Fashion Avenue. I wanted to see what the artsy crowd thought. But there were no seats and I was aggravated and didn't feel like asking anyone.

I boarded the train that evening and a woman sat down next to me. She was younger, more hip, and I thought she might buy my book. Then I said to myself, should I ask her? No! I'm not going to ask her. I'm not doing this anymore. I'm not asking fifty people for their opinions. I'm sticking to my original title!

A minute later, she pulled out a manuscript from her briefcase and started correcting it. *She turned out to be a book editor!*

Of course, I asked her opinion. She picked out my title.

She loved the idea for the cover and she said my back cover text was well written. Thank you, Lord.

I would like to take this time to thank all these women from the bottom of my heart.

A week before the book went to print, I was on my way to a restaurant called, Paradise, with my girlfriend Donna and she starting ragging on me about using a pen name. Marianne is my real first name. Thompson is the maiden name of my editor so I use that for my last name. I think it's very appropriate to have a pen name. It protects your privacy.

The restaurant was beautiful and situated right on the harbor in Stamford, Connecticut. Donna was to meet a casual blind date there. Shortly after we ordered drinks, he arrived and she began chatting with him. A few minutes later, unexpectedly, a guy she works with came up to us to say hello. He was with a friend.

I began talking about the launching of *Zapped* and how the book deals with the ramifications of growing up in an alcoholic home. Donna's blind date said, "My mother was an alcoholic." Then the next guy chimed in, "My dad was an alcoholic." And the last guy said, "My dad also was an alcoholic." We all shook our heads in amazement and started to laugh at the odd coincidence. Although it is not as odd as you might think considering what an epidemic alcoholism is.

We all continued talking, having a really good time, but after a while her friends from work had to leave. Keith handed me his card and told me what a pleasure it was to have met me. We hugged and bade farewell.

A few minutes after they left, I looked down at his business card and he had the same last name as me! His name is Keith Thompson! Donna and I thought this was hilarious. Shortly thereafter we left the restaurant, dropped her blind date off at the railroad station and, for some strange reason, we decided to go to the restaurant Baang in Greenwich. We rarely go there. When we walked in, who was there but Keith Thompson! We all went nuts.

When you meet someone by coincidence, it is suppose to be for a reason. I often thought I should dedicate this book to the adult children of alcoholics but for some reason it just slipped past me. Of course I also wanted to dedicate the book to Ron Allison because without him there would be no book. But my meeting with Keith Thompson showed me a dual dedication is the way to go. Thanks for the reminder God.

And speaking of Ron, he retired and left the church about a year and a half ago and moved back to the West Coast. I cried like a baby. And the tears are coming down this very minute as I type this tribute. He and his wife Penny had been away from their family for too long. Ron has been my biggest supporter and I will never be able to express how much I appreciate all he's done for me. He believed in me. That belief gave me the confidence and the courage I needed to finish this book. A priceless gift.

In talking about self-love, Ron once said, we can only love others as much as we love ourselves.

The most important thing in life is how you feel about yourself. I found myself and I love what I found. The spiritual experience I had has changed my life.

I quit smoking. It's been three and a half years since I had my last cigarette and I don't even miss it! And I smoked for twenty-five years. It went so well with the drinking.

I used to be chronically depressed but now, I rarely get

depressed. My self-esteem is up a thousand fold. My anxiety is at an all time low.

I conquered my demons! Most of them at least. Life still has its struggles. But the roads aren't as bumpy as they used to be. Life is at last, worth living.

After all God's done for me, I felt I had to give something back. For the last three years I've been doing volunteer work with the church.

I visit a woman who has multiple sclerosis. Her name is Melissa. She is bedridden. Forty years old. Her husband divorced her when she developed the illness and then moved to New Mexico with her two sons. Melissa has gotten everything in life that you don't want. But after all she's been through, she still has an amazing spirit and a wonderful sense of humor.

My main objective was to get Melissa out of the house. She lies in bed all day watching television. The highlight of her day is when her nurse's aides come to take care of her.

I asked Melissa one day, "Would you like to see a Broadway Play?"

"I'd love to. I've never been to one," she said.

We decided to go to *Cats* since it was the longest running play on Broadway and I had never been. I called the theater to make sure they were handicapped accessible. They were, so, I ordered the tickets. "That will be $7.50 for orchestra seats, for the person in the wheelchair and the companion," the ticket seller said and I almost fell off my chair. $7.50 for orchestra seats, anytime, any day for all major plays at the Shubert Theater! The moral of the story is Give and you Shall Receive. Melissa and I went to plays once a month. Then we went out for dinner. We struggled a little bit getting her in and out of the car but once we got her in, I'd throw the wheelchair in the backseat and off we'd go.

But Melissa's illness has deteriorated over the past three years. She used to be able to help when I got her in and out of the wheelchair. But now she can't. She has lost all her strength. So, we don't get to go to the plays anymore. We've seen most of them anyway.

Now the church pays for an ambulance to pick her up and we go to the mall to see the latest movies. It's been a wonderful experience helping Melissa. You get back what you give and develop a much greater appreciation for all the good things in your life.

And it seems when you find yourself you also discover hidden talents. Besides writing, I took up sculpting. I always wanted to sculpt, but I never did anything about it. One day my friend Maritza asked me if I wanted to take a course, Figure Modeling in Clay. We did and my sculpture came out really well. My teacher and I were both amazed! She thought I had taken sculpting classes before. I had a gut feeling that I'd be good at it and I was. I followed my intuitions.

And, there's a new man in my life. He's really the first true love of my life. The sweetest man I've ever known. It's been a real Cinderella story so far. He's tall and handsome and he's been a real Prince.

His name is Stanton, but I just call him Sweetie.

I took things very slowly this time. I made him wait. I got to know him and trust him before we became intimate.

He's unlike any other man I've dated. He calls me three times a day to tell me he loves me. He bought me a pearl necklace for our one-month anniversary, a diamond necklace for our two-month anniversary, and a very expensive shearling coat for our one-year anniversary! We celebrated our anniversary every month for the first year.

This was the *first time* in my life that I celebrated a solid one-year anniversary. And it has been the best year of my life.

All the expensive material things have been wonderful, but it's the little things that mean the most to me. When my car is low on gas, he fills it up and then has it washed. He's definitely the most thoughtful man I've ever known. One of the most touching moments was when I was out of toilet paper. He ran out and bought me two 24-roll packs! I think that's when I really fell in love with him.

He's never put me down. He doesn't have a temper, doesn't drink to excess. He's loyal and faithful. He's a real gentleman. Opens doors, stands when I get up from the table, helps me with my coat. Treats me like Gold.

I love him and he loves me. So stay tuned! And the next time you're *Zapped* always remember: There's no such thing as a coincidence, it's just God's way of remaining anonymous!

EPILOGUE

I'd like to say a few last words in *honor* of my mother. Throughout this book I have revealed her darkest side and now I would like to take this time to tell you the good things about my mother. She was a beautiful woman, tall and blonde, with long legs and porcelain skin. She wore Cherries in Snow lipstick and Chanel No.5 perfume. Besides being beautiful she was also an extremely intelligent woman, an avid bridge player and crossword puzzle fanatic.

She had a great laugh. She would laugh so hard at my father's jokes. Sometimes we didn't know if she was laughing with him or at him. There was always comic relief in our house.

She was an excellent cook –– best lasagna ever created by an Irish woman. Usually at Christmas she would gather all of us in the kitchen. A little assembly line preparing all the different parts to the lasagna.   One of us would be cutting the mozzarella, not too thick, not too thin, cut in perfect even little squares. And while the best sauce in the world was simmering, someone else would be rolling the meatballs. Instead of the traditional meat sauce we would have to roll these very tiny meatballs for our lasagna piling them high on plates getting them ready for the frying pan. I always used to brag to my Italian friends about the little meatballs we had in our lasagna. Can you imagine, the Italians were jealous of our lasagna. Yep, my mother made mean lasagna.

She also had a talent for nutty fingers. Little crescent shaped butter and pecan cookies. When she took them out of the oven we got to roll them in confectioners sugar. Deelish! And one Christmas she made a Santa Claus cake. My sister and I sat in utter amazement staring at this huge Santa head with red cap, coconut pom-pom and a coconut beard. It was the only cake ever I didn't want to eat.

She knew the value of education. "You can't depend on a man," "A girl without skills is a Dead Duck," she used to say. And she was right. When I had dropped out of college and was floundering, she would bug me every day. "What are you going to do with your life?'" "You have to go back to school." She forced me to get a career. Unfortunately, I was the one who chose the Fashion Industry.

Religion was also very important to her. Sunday was always a special day. We went to church every Sunday, then right afterwards we would make the traditional pit stop at Dunkin' Donuts and later in the evening she made a big Sunday dinner. The only bad part about Sunday was we had to watch the Lawrence Welk Show at night.

My cousin Pam speaks very highly of my mother. At Sweeties' birthday party she started to cry when she spoke of her and said, "I know you had problems with your mother but I loved Aunt Mary. Every holiday she would send us presents. On Halloween, Easter and Christmas. When we saw the UPS man coming up the driveway, we knew it was a gift from Aunt Mary. And the gifts would be wrapped so beautifully. At Christmas she would tie candy canes to the bows and inside the package she would always give us a nice sweater or new outfit but then extra treats would be inside. Like those waxed lips or harmonica candy. Or candy necklaces and tootsie roll pops. I loved your mother."

She was a good woman, but somehow she got lost. I wish she could have found her way back. It's very sad the way my mother's life ended.

After one of my strange and wondrous coincidences a friend once remarked, "I think your mother is your guardian angel today." Perhaps that friend is right and somehow my mother's spirit has guided me into coming to terms with the effect her disease had on me. With understanding and for-giveness of the past I have become a whole person. And if it weren't for my mother, who brought me into this world...I wouldn't be able to give testimony to what a wonderful life it is! I love you Mom. The best guardian angel a girl could ever ask for.